How to Select and Raise your

ULTIMATE DOG

Gaz Jackson

How to Select and Raise your ULTIMATE DOG
© Gaz Jackson 2015
Third Edition

Front Cover Dog Trainer and Author Gaz Jackson with (from left to right):
Chance, Australia's first cancer detection dog trained to detect breast and skin cancers from sweat patches.
Oscar, Australia's first koala detection dog trained to locate koalas in trees to assist ecologists in koala protection. Tragically Oscar was hit by a car and killed whilst indicating on a stunned koala in the middle of the road. Tribute video on YouTube channel.
Maya, Australia's first koala scat detection dog trained to locate poop to find koala populations. Now working full time for the University of the Sunshine Coast Detection Dogs for Conservation.
Migaloo, the world's first archaeology dog is trained to find ancient human remains including Aboriginal sacred sites for the elders. Migaloo is also the world record holder for the oldest human remains find in history for a detection dog of a carbon-dated 600-year-old skeleton

National Library of Australia Cataloguing-in-Publication entry (pbk)

Author:	Jackson, G. (Gaz) author
Title:	How to Select and Raise your ULTIMATE DOG / Gaz Jackson
ISBN:	978-1-925680-03-4 (paperback)
Subjects:	Dogs--Training
Dewey Number:	636.70835

Published by Gaz Jackson and Ocean Reeve Publishing
www.oceanreeve.com.au

REEVE
PUBLISHING

Foreword

The continued presence of the domestic dog in our lives seems so ordinary to us that we perhaps don't realise what a remarkable phenomenon the dog is. These animals have lived side-by-side with human beings for 20,000 years or more. They possess a unique genetic heritage that, in combination with domestication and selective breeding, has produced a mind-boggling range of different shapes, sizes, and colours of dogs, with an even more mind-boggling range of different behavioural properties.

Endemic nearly world-over in the countryside and in rural settings, dogs are numerous and ordinary inhabitants of most of the urban centers in the world, and they have begun to make their appearance even in societies and cities where they were formerly absent or rare. For instance, just as millions of well-off Chinese have begun to take up Western habits of consumption where automobiles and clothing and wrist-watches are concerned, many thousands of them have also taken up dog ownership. It is possible to drive down a street in Beijing, as I did in 2006, and encounter a long row of neat, vaguely Western-style homes with fenced yards and fine, impressive dogs trotting the fences and barking their announcements.

Wherever they are kept, however, dogs are rarely given the consideration they deserve, and decisions regarding dogs are not given the importance that they should be, in the name of both human and dog welfare. Dog purchases (or acquisitions, when money does not change hands) tend to be based on impulse, whim, fashion, by accident, or due to misinformation. Few people, even those that appreciate that a dog is a living, breathing, uncannily intelligent animal capable (most would argue) of a range of emotions (contentment, discomfort, pain, fear, happiness, joy) similar to our own. Few people also appreciate that a healthy dog will live a major portion of a human being's life span. Few of us stop to think that during a dog's twelve or fifteen years of life, the animal's presence in its owner's life will, if the dog is well cared for and well used, impose very significant burdens. These burdens are of all kinds—liability to friends and family and neighbours via noise and mess and potential dog bites, loss of sleep, and time spent caring for the dog (especially when the animal is very young or very old), thought and planning for integrating the dog into lifestyle and career and schedule, and (not least) the raw monetary expense of owning a dog, feeding it, providing it with medical care (sometimes shockingly dear), replacing the things it destroys, etc.

In the best case, these burdens of dog ownership are richly offset by the joy and the contentment of living with an 'ultimate dog'; a dog that one loves, that is compatible with one's temperament and situation and lifestyle, a dog that gets one out to walk or exercise or socialise or breathe the air, a being that keeps one company, never criticises one, makes one feel a little more secure, or whatever your ultimate dog does for you. But this, as with all things in life, is an equation that may weigh more heavily on one side than the other. When all is well, the benefits of owning a dog heavily outweigh the burdens, and this happens often enough that many millions of us spend our lives owning a succession of dogs that are precious to us. But in many other cases, unfortunately and even sometimes tragically, the burdens outweigh the benefits, sometimes with long-lasting and far-reaching costs to the owner, to the dog, and to the society harbouring dog and owner.

The thing that my colleague and friend Gaz Jackson (and the author of this book) realises is that acquiring a dog is a very important and serious decision. The long-term outcome in terms of weighing burden against benefit is very much a function of the wisdom, knowledge, judgment, and caution that are exercised while making the decision to acquire or not acquire a dog, and deciding what kind of dog to acquire and how to care for it, keep it, and train it.

What we need when the misty-eyed impulse to acquire a dog strikes us is some no-nonsense advice. I am no exception, even after thirty-five years with dogs. Recently while on a business trip in the Netherlands, I came perilously close to making the wildly inappropriate and probably very expensive decision to purchase an eight-week-old Dutch Shepherd named Bonnie, a very special daughter of the very special Netherlands working sire Big Roy Pegge. The purchase proved impossible, and when I came to my senses I was so glad!

What we need and get in this book is no-nonsense, unvarnished advice from an expert who cares about both dogs and people, who has seen enough to grasp the essential facts about dog ownership, and who is not afraid to put them across in simple, un-sugared, and sometimes not completely politically correct terms. In this very useful and to-the-point book, that expert is Gaz Jackson, a man younger than I but with tremendously broad experience with dogs and dog training and who, I believe, has indeed seen damn near everything under the sun where dogs are concerned. I commend him to those who are considering acquiring a dog, and at the very least if everyone in the world took the trouble to read this book, and took the necessary pause for thought and consideration before they acquired a dog, the world would be a better place for dogs, and probably for people as well.

Stewart Hilliard, PhD
San Antonio, Texas
September, 2015

Contents

Chapter 8

Introduction

I've been a full-time professional dog trainer for over thirty years, training in excess of 20,000 dogs and dealing with thousands of people in the dog industry. I have just about seen it all.

My mission is to make this book extremely informative and totally unbiased in every way, without motives based on the opinions of other dog groups' views.

I will show you the secrets of professional dog trainers and how to get the most out of your dog and how to deal with breeders and dog dealers so that you are armed with knowledge and the tricks of the trade before you select your new dog.

I cover in the book the details of finding and selecting your ultimate dog or selecting an adult dog for immediate testing and training. I cover all the problems you may experience with your new dog and outline how to fix them.

I will give you factual information on many things, from electric collars to check chains. I will present you with the facts on how and why a particular training item is used and its good qualities when used correctly and its bad qualities when used incorrectly.

I will also give you alternative options and, finally, my professional opinion based on over thirty years of dog training experience.

Because I cover such items as electric collars in my book, welfare organisations may not promote this book, as some information goes against the beliefs of the organisation. You can give people within these organisations scientific facts about check chains and electronic collars and they will still refuse to believe them; they will continue to believe the biased views of their organisation.

I will give you the facts and you can make up your own mind and empower yourself with great knowledge so that you can start your journey in selecting and training your ultimate dog.

I am certain that if you apply the knowledge in this book you will be able to find and select your ultimate dog.

Gaz Jackson

Chapter 1

Before You Begin

I am just about to write my first entry in the first chapter of my first book. I am in San Antonio, Texas, USA, where I'm visiting a good friend of mine, Dr Stewart Hilliard, at Lackland Air Force Base. Dr Hilliard holds a PhD in animal learning, and for the last fifteen years he has worked with and for the United States Department of Defense Military Working Dog Program, which has its' so-called 'schoolhouse' at Lackland. The military base houses up to 1000 military dogs that are in training for explosives detection and other specialist areas. The facility is incredible, with everything you could possibly need to train dogs, from the five plane fuselages mounted on pillars used for search training, to the compound filled with dozens and dozens of automobiles for hiding target odours, and the many buildings all decked out for different search scenarios, to the large scent-detection rooms. To get the dogs from kennel to training ground the air force has a large fleet of dual-cab F250s with eighteen-berth air-conditioned dog trailers.

The dogs used are mostly German Shepherd dogs, but with many Belgian Malinois, and even a few sporting dog breeds. The majority of the dogs are bred or selected from top breeders and dealers in Europe, but Dr. Hilliard also runs a small program to breed and rear specially-selected Belgian Malinois at Lackland to become military working dogs. The best products of this Department of Defense Military Working Dog Breeding Program are dogs of a quality that are very difficult to find on the open

3

market. These are the kind of ultimate dogs the US military require for their work.

***

You're not just given an ultimate dog; the ultimate dog depends on a combination of several aspects. Let's take a look at some that the US military may consider pretty important.

1. Selecting the best breed for the job.
2. Selecting the best working dogs within that breed.
3. Selecting the best breeding programs from around the world.
4. Selecting the best breeders and dealers.
5. Developing a puppy foster care program to develop and prepare the pups for military training.
6. Having a state of the art facility for care and training of the dogs.
7. Having some of the world's top military working dog trainers and behaviourists on staff.
8. Having the most advanced dog training programs to prepare dogs for military service.
9. Having a comprehensive handler training program so both handler and dog can work as a highly effective team.
10. Being able to maintain the training standard to ensure both dog and handler maintain a high standard.

Many dog units will have their own programs for breeding, training, and operational procedures, to get the best results. When you combine the combination of knowledge and research you are well on your way to getting your ultimate dog.

You can be a very talented trainer with a great connection with dogs, but if the dog you choose has the wrong temperament or has been exposed to bad experiences or lacks socialisation, you will have a very small chance at achieving your ultimate dog. I have seen so many people try to work with a dog that was not suitable in the first place but they will try to try to get the results, which will always end in disappointment. I have also seen many people who are bad handlers and do all the wrong things with their dog and yet the dog has turned out great mostly due to the breeding and character of the dog.

So let's get down to business. You may be reading this because you want the best dog possible and you need some guidance and advice from a veteran dog trainer to help you get there.

In the past you have been bombarded with information and advice by everyone from family and friends to so-called experts or people who are so obsessed with their breed of dog that they push their opinions onto you. Dog trainers might also push their methods and beliefs onto you. It seems that every person you talk to about a dog is an expert and their last dog was Rin-Tin-Tin or Lassie, or they are good friends with the country's greatest dog trainer.

So now let's talk about you and what you want from a dog. You love dogs and would love to have your own personal companion that loves you and that you can be proud of. You may be a big dog lover or you may work in the dog industry as a vet nurse or animal control officer.

You are still deciding on your favourite breed; you had the most awesome dog as a child and you love that breed, or your buddy had a really cool, well-trained dog. Do you get a dog that is really popular at the moment or a small dog that is easy to handle? What about the amount of time you'll have to put in to training? Do you get a pup or an adult, a male or a female? You've heard funny things about this breed or that breed, but are they true? Do you employ a professional trainer or go to the local obedience school? There are so many decisions to make!

Before we go on, grab a pen and write down now the details of your ultimate dog. We will see how much these details change after you have read the book.

Breed_____

Male or female_____

Puppy or adult_____

What am I going to train for?_____

Personality and manners_____

Important things I want my dog to do_____

Now let's start with the joy of having an awesome dog and dream about what it would be like. This is to help you on your journey and inspire you. What do you want in a dog in training, looks, personality, and day-to-day living?

Maybe you love to see a magnificently bred dog that looks very stunning and is confident and powerful, a dog that is highly social and protective. Maybe you love a crossbred toy dog with a huge smile and loads of energy. You see, your ultimate dog is the dog that you love and that appeals to you, not anyone else. I am here to guide you, with information and suggestions to help you achieve this goal.

Here are some examples of what three people think is their ultimate dog.

I Dream of My Ultimate Dog

Geoffrey Pearce
Retired male in his 60s living on acreage.

"I have been on my own for twenty years and my only companion is my dog, who is my best mate. The looks aren't that important to me but the personality is. My two crossbreds have a smile from ear to ear and they love me so much. They will sleep by my bed each night and stay with me in the lounge during the day. Both dogs are great watchdogs so they will run to the fence and bark at anyone that walks past. They are both very affectionate and love chasing birds in the back paddock. I really enjoy sitting back and watching them do what dogs do, from wrestling each other, to digging a hole, to sleeping at my feet after a big day. They are my family and I treat them like my children and I love them so much."

Adam Sessions
Ex-federal policeman now full-time canine security guard in his 40s

"My ultimate dog would be a German shepherd of Czechoslovakian and East German bloodlines. This combination provides extreme drive and aggression with a balance of calmness and sharpness required in a working dog. The dog must be of medium build for strength and agility, and would be in a black sable. He would be fearless, with great defence for extreme display and protective qualities, but also have a great prey drive for off-lead attacks and tracking, etc. He would also have a great suspicion trigger with fast recovery."

Paul Martin
Veteran security dog handler, dog breeder/ trainer

"I have being a canine handler in the security industry for over a decade and in that time I had the pleasure of working with two dogs—both Belgian Malinois. These were my ultimate dogs; lean, well-proportioned, but with this great muscle tone that only the Malinois seem to have. The drive to work and work, hard, strong-willed, yet always eager to please once trained to a level that they knew exactly what you wanted from them in sticky situations; and there were plenty. I never once feared that they would falter. These dogs seemed almost indestructible, ready, but not frothing at the mouth nor out of control, and with one word they would demonstrate the exact command that was given. What more to say? They are the ultimate working dog."

Gaz Jackson

Which Dog Breed is Best for Me?

The first step is to work out what your end game is; in other words, is your ultimate dog going to be a family pet or a working dog for security or detection work? Once you have this information we can then start to narrow down the breeds suitable for what you want. Other factors that can influence your decision is past experience from watching dogs on television, having a childhood pet, or having a friend with a highly trained working dog. You may live in an apartment but your favourite dog is a Great Dane.

Let's say, as an example, you want a dog as a family pet only. Do you live in a house or apartment, or on acreage? What time do you have each day to spend with your dog? Do you have an active or inactive lifestyle?

Starting off, with every breed available you will find that all dogs are suitable to own if you have acreage or a backyard. When the size of your accommodation is down to a unit or apartment, you will be better suited to a small- to medium-sized dog, from any of the toy breeds to dogs such as Staffordshire terriers, pugs, French bulldogs, poodles, and even some larger types such as collies, Labradors, and golden retrievers.

I would like to point out that not all dogs of an individual breed are the same. You can have working line dogs and show line dogs and they will be like chalk and cheese. A working dog may have stronger character and be super energetic with high retrieval drive to chase a ball or a stick. These dogs are the best for training but can be a handful to live with.

If you want a dog to sit around all day, a dog like this may not be the dog for you. The show line or pet quality dogs generally have a softer character and limited or low drives and are best suited as family pets. Mismatches can be made very easily so it's important not only to select the right breed, but the right dog within the breed.

You may be searching for a working dog to train for a specific talent, such as personal protection in law enforcement, detection dog training, or herding.

Let's look at personal protection training for your home or business—or maybe you are a professional law enforcement officer and require a dog for your employment. The best breeds for these purposes are German shepherd, Belgian Malinois, Rottweiler, Doberman, and Rhodesian ridgeback. Many other breeds are suitable including bull mastiff, Neapolitan mastiff, or pit bull, however many agencies have strict breed specifications so the other dogs may be excluded but will still work well in other applications.

Take note that your ultimate dog may be a personal protection Neapolitan mastiff, but if you are doing a lot of walking on patrol the dog won't keep up so it will not be suitable for your application. This is also the same if you have a high energy dog that can keep up but is soft of character and cannot be trained in protection.

If it is a detection dog you are looking for then the best breeds are Belgian shepherd, German shepherd, Labrador, golden retriever, Border collie, or Springer spaniel. Many more purebred and cross-bred dogs are suitable so you need to get the right one for the application. I have used Manchester terriers for cane toad detection and fox terriers for breast cancer detection and both have been excellent but are not suitable in other detection applications.

If you wish to cross-train your dog, as many police and military departments do in, for example, personal protection and narcotic detection, then it may be best to stick with Belgian Malinois and German shepherd breeds.

In search and rescue the best by far is the bloodhound, but most large breeds can be used—as long as they have the agility and the drive, you can train them to search.

In conclusion, you know your favourite dog, and it will be a bonus if your favourite dog also fits into your training requirements. This may be your only compromise as you may love poodles but require a personal protection dog. With research you will be able to bring these together by going for your second or third choice so that the breed fits your needs.

Do I Get a Male or a Female?

I have worked with thousands of males and females in different applications and YES, there is a big difference between the males and females. You will firstly have to choose what you want to train your dog for and the pros and cons of living with a male or female. Let's firstly look at living with a male dog. In a lot of cases the male will develop, as he reaches adolescence, a protective or territorial state on the property he lives on.

Take into account that if the male was highly socialised with people then the dog will be a great social dog but may still bark and put on a territorial show for people behind the fence. If the male is with a female then he may establish himself as the rank leader of the pack and become more protective over his pack and territory. The male may start marking his home by urinating around the property, such as on the fence-line, and kicking up the ground he urinated on to spread his odour.

When the male becomes protective of the property he may see not only humans as a threat, but other dogs and wild native animals such as foxes as well. At a later stage the frustration of barking behind a fence will increase his aggression levels and you can end up with a dog that wants to chase wildlife and other dogs. I will get more into this later into the book and how to avoid these problems.

I consistently find that females are more chilled out and easier to live with without the territorial marking that some males will do. Also note that this above example is not representative of all male and female dogs. If you have genetically soft character dogs that are well-socialised, both the male and female will be pleasures to live with.

If you select a hard character working line dog with heaps of drive, both male and female will have a lot of energy and will not slow down. These dogs are generally very active and will chew, dig, and bark at everything—anything to relieve their unlimited energy. This is because of the genetic working dog base. Now if you add to this no socialisation, then you will end up with a high energy dog with high suspicion levels and the dog will become even harder to live with.

If your aim is to have a protection dog for home or as a working law enforcement dog, I recommend a male dog. I have seen many litters where the males have turned out to be great working dogs whereas the females from the same litter have failed or been very average without the hardness of their male brothers.

A large amount of females that are successful protection dogs are mostly working in prey drive, without much defence. There are many females that have made excellent protection dogs in personal, sport, and law enforcement capacities, but as a trainer testing out thousands of dogs over many years I have found the males to be the better protective gender when compared to the females.

If your aim is to have a working detection dog, then both male and female are both suitable for this application. I always avoid hard character dogs when I select a dog for detection as it creates too many problems in training, such as territorial marking, which can distract from the detection work. However, if I required a multi-purpose dog for protection and detection, I would select a male or, if available, an exceptional female.

I have trained a lot of environmental detection dogs and I find the best to use are females, as you have much less drama with marking and dominance issues so you can concentrate on detection training. I have also used strong character males, and a large amount of time went into fixing dominance issues with these. I found that soft character males with high drive have made excellent environmental detection dogs.

So, in summary, the best dog to live with would be a female or a softer character male. For any protection work I would choose a male and for detection I would choose a female of high drive or a soft character male. The hardest dogs to live with are hard character working line dogs.

I have seen so many people that will select the best-bred dog and pay large amounts of money for this world class breeding, to end up with a dog version of a seven-year-old child with ADHD. The most common complaint is that a dog just doesn't slow down and is jumping on everyone because it is always excited, barks at everything, and chews anything lying around. This kind of dog is genetically a very hard character dog and it also has a very high pain threshold so when the owner tries to take the dog for a walk they are dragged down the street and no amount of yelling at the dog seems to work.

Do I Choose a Puppy or an Adult?

By now you should have a good idea of what breed to get that is suitable for your living and training needs, and whether to get a male or a female. Now the big question is 'do I get a puppy or an adult dog?'.

There are pros and cons in both pups and adults and later we will go over a lot of details to help you choose where you will get your puppy or adult dog from.

Firstly we will look at the advantages and disadvantages of getting a puppy compared with an adult dog. In Chapters 2 and 3 I cover a lot of information on puppies and where to start looking, and in Chapter 4, how to raise and develop your pup into a great young adult. In Chapters 5 and 6 I cover where to search to locate an adult dog and how to develop the dog in preparation for training. I also cover how to evaluate and test potential puppies or adult dogs for suitability for your lifestyle and training requirements.

There are so many breeders and dealers of puppies and most will tell you what you want to hear with many self-proclaimed experts claiming their pups are the best. The first few months of a puppy's life make up the critical period and there are plenty of studies that have been done on this timeframe. I could write a book just on this period alone, but here I will simply outline some of the most important stuff.

When the puppies are born their eyes are closed so they rely heavily on their sense of smell and touch by having lots of contact with their littermates and their mother. During this time the pup has now worked out a scent picture. The puppy's eyes will open after around nine to fourteen days' time, followed by the ears. As they reach one month of age, puppies are gradually weaned and begin to eat solid food.

The mother may regurgitate partially digested food for the puppies or might let them eat some of her solid food. In the timeframe starting at around four weeks to eight weeks the pups will be interacting with the littermates, playing tug-o-war, chewing, and developing as social animals. This period is so important for a puppy and it should remain with the mother till at least seven weeks or ideally eight weeks of age.

Do not take a puppy before at least seven weeks of age. You may be thinking, 'Now this is not such a big deal, it's only a week.' Let me explain what may happen if a puppy is taken away too early from the mother or if the puppy remains with the mother for too long.

During the period before the puppy's eyes are open the puppy has a great scent picture of the mother's smell and the smell of its littermates. This scent picture becomes a pacifier or comforter for the puppy. So the puppy now associates this smell with the touch and drink from the mother. At four to six weeks of age the puppy has eyes and ears open and is very dependent on the mother. The puppy will find it difficult to rest unless it is wallowing in the mother's scent pool and the touch and body heat of the mother and the littermates.

This is why if you separate a puppy from the mother and the litter in this period they will find it hard to settle and may start crawling to search for the mother, or sit and whine. When the puppy is put back in the litter it will most likely immediately settle. When a puppy is removed from the litter at, for example, four or five weeks of age and given to the new owner, a series of behaviours will take place. The dependency the puppy had on the mother and the littermates will transfer to the new owner, so the first few nights will be unbearable until the puppy's dependency transfers completely to you. The dependency will be compounded if the puppy is allowed to sleep in your bedroom, so by the time the puppy is eight weeks of age you may have a very insecure and dependent puppy that will bring you a lot of stress and have many behaviour problems.

If the puppy is left with the mother and littermates till around four months of age, the puppy will also become severely dependent due to the fact that the puppy has missed out on the critical stage of development in the socialisation period that should occur before sixteen weeks of age. The second problem is that during this time the puppy has never been on its own so cannot and more than likely will not cope without undergoing stress. As a result of remaining with the litter and mother till sixteen weeks of age when the puppy is placed into a new home, the dependency will transfer again to the new owner.

So taking the puppy away from the mother and littermates before seven weeks of age or after sixteen weeks of age will create an overly dependent dog. Environmental factors that will compound the problems are bad experiences like been frightened by a dog or stranger, or sleeping in the owner's bedroom.

Now this is what will happen with a dog that is dependent on the new owner: because the dog's pacifier is wallowing in the scent pool of the mother, this will now transfer to the new owner. The puppy will follow you around everywhere you go and will always be under your feet and around you. The dependent pup will be totally relaxed when asleep within your scent pool, so when you sit down the puppy will lay down under your feet to go to sleep, when you move the puppy will follow, and the puppy will not settle until it is in your scent pool. As this is a big pacifier for the dog the dependency will cause the dog to always stick its nose in your crotch or armpit or mouth, as these areas have the heaviest odour bases. The dependent dog may also be a chronic licker, always licking your legs and arms to gather more odour. When you are away the dog's stress levels will go up and the dog will pace, sniff under the door to get your odour, or find your odour around the house, such as in dirty laundry, shoes, pillows, or anything else you have touched. As the dog is under stress it may start howling or barking or start destructive chewing.

The second part of the dependency is separation anxiety. This is when the dog starts barking or howling when you go out and will pace back and forth, panting very quickly, with shallow breathing. As its anxiety is high the dog will have much higher suspicion levels and may respond by barking at everything. The dog will sit at the fence at the next point it will see you, which is usually the side yard, or the dog may dig a hole to lay in to keep cool and its ears will be focused on the road outside and will hear your car from two blocks away.

The third stage is the dog becoming overprotective and starting to see all people and animals as a threat to the rank structure. In this stage if you have a hard character working dog, the chances are much higher the dog will start growling at people or being aggressive from behind the fence. In the early stages the dog will start to circle the owner and sit on your feet, looking at the stranger, followed by flattening his against its head and growling. Other ways the dog will try to establish itself as rank number two to you, the owner as rank number one, will be to urinate on the stranger's odour.

So get your puppy at around eight weeks of age and socialise your dog heavily. Taking the puppy too early or too late, getting a dog that has had a bad experience, or allowing your dog to sleep in the bedroom may create a dog that becomes dependent, has separation anxiety, and is over-protective. This is then followed by a lifetime of other behaviour problems. Chapter 3 will cover the puppy tests so that you can be sure to pick a winner.

The biggest advantage of starting off with an eight-week-old puppy is that you can develop a great bond and start moulding the puppy to your lifestyle and training program, and if you know how to raise and develop a puppy you will end up with an awesome adult dog that is social and obedient and developed as a working dog.

You can raise a dog perfectly, but if the puppy has the wrong genetic base you will not end up with your ultimate dog. It is important that you have the correct breeding and breed for what you want in a dog, then if you raise it well you will get your super dog.

Now let's look at the advantages of securing an adult dog that is either trained or untrained.

The biggest advantage is that you see your adult dog as an adult and can identify some of the tricks it has learnt throughout its life. You can either get an adult untrained dog that you can evaluate for suitability for you, or purchase an adult dog from a trainer who has already trained the dog. Many people prefer this way as they can see what they are getting on the spot when it comes to the looks and ability of the dog. The other advantage is that if you require a dog for a security crisis or for employment you can have one working with you within a week or even as little as a day. Purchase of an adult dog is suitable for all applications from a pet to a detection or protection dog.

On the negative side, you lose the joy of raising a pup into an adult and you may also end up with a series of problems caused by the last owner. For example, the dog may not be socialised or the owner may have punished the dog by hitting it with rolled up newspaper, causing shyness. There can be many problems and some you won't see till after you live with the dog for a while.

So, as you can see, there are advantages and disadvantages when choosing a puppy at eight weeks of age or a young adult at fourteen months. I personally prefer to evaluate a young adult so I know exactly what I have with an evaluation, and I can start training straight away. In some cases the dog gets half-way through the training program and then fails, so I can rehome the dog and start again with another candidate.

If this happened with a pup you raised, you would have wasted twelve months of raising a pup to a young adult, only to find out it didn't live up to your expectations. Most people that have been in this situation end up keeping the failed dog because they have developed such a strong bond, and so end up with a pet with limited training potential.

By now you should be closer to making a decision on the type of training you want for your ultimate dog. You should have an idea of the breed that will best suit your training and lifestyle, the desired sex of your dog, and finally, whether you should get a puppy or an adult.

Gaz Jackson

What Are the Costs of Buying and Owning a Dog?

Owning a dog is a big, long-term commitment, as your new puppy may live to be ten to fifteen years of age. So let's get straight to the point on the expected costs of owning a pet or a working dog.

Purchase of Your Dog

You may be lucky to get your dog as a giveaway, or only pay a small amount of money to a rescue service for your pet. The costs of purchasing a dog will vary from 'free to good home' to $1000 for a highly sought after purebred. The average price I see for the rescue dogs is around $400, which will also include the de-sexing and vaccinations. If you decide to go down the track of getting a puppy from a breeder, then you could be looking at a minimum of $800. Backyard breeders may have pups available for around $200. High quality pups from imported lines may be between $1000 and $3000 each, with rare breeds being even more expensive. On average, allow $1000 for a pet and $2500 for a highly bred pup from a breeder.

Getting Your Home Set Up for Your Dog

You will have to have all the basics from your local pet store including food and water bowls, toys, bedding, and also all your training equipment from collars and leads. The total cost of this will be around $200 and for high-end products around $500. You may need specialist equipment for future training, which may include leather harnesses, leads, tracking equipment, or protection gear from body bite suits to sleeves. For all your specialist training gear stay away from your local pet store and only get the high quality equipment made from specialist suppliers, or have them custom-made. High quality leads and collars start at around $100 and can be as high as $400. Sleeves start at $250 and body bite suits start at $2000. As well as all the basics you will also need to have a secure area for the dog, which may mean that you will have to build a dog run and kennel, which may be around $1000, and have dog-proof fencing that can be anywhere from $20 to $200 per metre depending on materials used.

Veterinary Care

There is an ongoing cost for annual vaccinations and worming, which will cost at least $200 per year. You will also encounter the inevitable emergency visit to the vet which may be as little as $200 or over $1000 if you go on a public holiday. Maintenance of your dog will include flea and tick prevention and regular hydrobaths at $50 to $100.

Diet

There is a big difference between the basic to the top-shelf diets for dogs. If you want your ultimate dog, don't skimp on the diet. On the lower end of the scale you have home brand supermarket dog biscuits that work out to be around $1.50 per kilo up to the high end working dog formulas at around $5 to $8 per kilo.

Training

This will vary greatly as you can invest in obedience classes starting at $20 per class or professional in-kennel training starting at $500 per week or professional private lessons ranging from $80 to $800 a private lesson.

Now let's crunch the numbers and get a total cost of owning a dog from an eight-week-old puppy to when the dog passes at, on average, ten years of age. I will also look at two scenarios, one that considers the budget pet owner and one that considers the professional who wants the best.

Example 1: The Budget Dog Owner

The budget dog owner got their puppy as a giveaway and went to the local pet store to buy cheap dog gear totalling $100 and this was replaced every year for ten years: $1000.

Veterinary maintenance for vaccinations and worming cost $200 per year, so $2000 for the ten-year period. The budget dog owner got cheap supermarket food at $1 per kilo, using half a kilo each day, totalling 182.5 kilos and $182.50 per year. So that's $1825 over ten years.

On the training side, the budget dog owner did it all themselves, so no costs there at all.

The total expenditure of the budget pet owner over the ten-year period was $4825 or $482.50 per year, or $9.27 per week, or $1.30 per day.

Example 2: The Professional

The professional researched and got the top-of-the-line breed from excellent breeders and paid $3000 for their new puppy. The professional also bought top-range gear such as stainless steel bowls, leather collars and leads, and high quality bedding and kennel, costing $1000. Only some of the gear was replaced during the ten-year period, at $500.

The professional got the best medication for vaccinations and worming and also did regular check-ups on their dog. This cost $400 per year or $4000 over ten years. The professional's dog only had the best diet of food that cost $6 per kilo, consuming half a kilo a day or 182.5 kilos per year, totalling $1095 or $10950 over ten years.

On the training side of things the professional did most of the training themselves; however they hired out another professional to put the dog through three lots of fourteen-day programs over three years, costing $800 per fourteen-day program or $2400 in total.

The total expenditure of the professional dog owner over the ten-year period was $21850 or $2185 per year, or $42.00 per week, or $6.00 per day.

	Budget	Professional	Difference
Ten-year cost	$4825:00	$21850:00	$17025:00
Annual cost	$482:50	$2185:00	$1702:50
Weekly cost	$9:27	$42:00	$32:73
Daily cost	$1:30	$6:00	$4:70

The above two scenarios should give you an approximate idea of the expected base costs of owning a dog and it is important that you know this before you go out and get a new dog, as it is a ten-year commitment that will cost you, on average, between $5000 and $20,000.

How Do I Prepare My Home for My New Dog?

Some people can be totally unprepared for this and others will spend a lot of time and money ensuring their house is pet-friendly. There are also many things that your new puppy will get into that will be totally unexpected.

Remember that when you bring your eight-week-old puppy home, the pup is in the middle of the most critical development period of its life. The timeframe up to around sixteen weeks of age is called the critical period because it *is* critical. The pup is taken from its litter and mother, handled by yourself, put into a cage or on the back seat of the car, and driven to your home.

The pup may be stressed being away from the litter and smelling all these new smells from you and your car so the pup's brain is working hard to figure all of this out. Finally the pup is at your home and handled by the family so the pup is now exhausted and tries to sleep but is stressed with new smells and no littermates to smell or touch. Over the next few weeks it is so important that the pup is developing in confidence and having many good experiences. The worst thing that can happen during this critical period is for the puppy to have terrible experiences that hurt or frighten it, such as being attacked by a dog or smacked. In Chapter 4 I will cover in detail how to raise a puppy and ensure it has the best start in life.

Now let's look at some steps to take to prepare your house for your new puppy.

Sleeping Area

As the puppy is now away from its litter it may be under stress and will start whingeing, and as a result the owner will pick it up or have the dog sleep on the bed with the owner or on the floor of the bedroom. This is the worst thing you can do; do not let your new puppy sleep with you in the bedroom, and I'll explain more about this later in the book. The best area for the puppy to sleep at night is inside the house secured in a room such as the laundry, which is rich with all the family's odours in the dirty clothes basket. The outside area may be the back patio or an enclosed garage. If the pup is around you all the time then the dog will stress when it is on its own, so this is the perfect chance to condition your pup to spend the night every night on its own.

I recommend you buy a pet transport cage for your pup to sleep in. Inside the cage place a comfortable mat or pillow for the puppy to sleep on with an odour base such as a sweaty shirt that belongs to you. On the inside door of the cage you can hang a water bowl and even have a treat or a toy to keep the pup occupied. Playing soft music at bedtime will also condition the pup with an association and soon the pup will calm very quickly when it is placed in the cage. The transport cage can be placed in the laundry or you can place it in an area when the pup can hear the family and the television. If you have an outdoor area you can also place the puppy out there on the first night, but try to have it secured to a small area so the pup doesn't go exploring and end up lost or stuck.

In summary, crate training your puppy from the first night, giving it a smelly shirt of the owner, and playing soft music will calm the pup—a small treat will also help. Conditioning the pup to spend time on its own will also help to avoid dependency problems.

Feeding Area

In nearly every household the feeding area of the dogs is at the back sliding door or on the kitchen floor. This then becomes an area the dog hangs around all day. The dog then rarely uses the rest of the property as they are constantly staring at the owner through the glass and waiting for the next feed. In the first few weeks of feeding a new puppy, I will associate the feeding with a room such as the laundry, so that when you prepare the pup's feed the pup will run ahead of you and wait at the feeding station. This is why when you feed your pup at the back door you are adding to the excitement of the pup wanting a feed every time you walk out and it goes crazy, jumping on you. Buy high quality stainless steel bowls for feeding that are put away when not in use. I will always have two water bowls with one placed under the garden tap and the other next to the food bowl outside. I always place the water bowl away from the back door so the pup has to walk to the back of the patio to get a drink.

Fences

It is so important to have a puppy- and dog-proof fence. The height of your fence for a puppy can be three feet high and for an adult six feet will usually do the trick, however some dogs can easily scale a six-foot fence. The bottom of the fence should be close enough to the ground that the pup cannot fit its head under it. If the desire is there the pup may attempt to dig out, so to secure the bottom of the fence-line here are some tips that may help:

- For smaller backyards you can cut sheets of mesh into strips of one foot and lay this down on the base of the fence, flat on the ground. You can bend a few inches of the mesh to make a right angle and nail it to the base of the fence, or keep it flat and secure it with tent pegs or weights, such as rocks. This will also work around chicken coops by lying flat mesh, or even chicken wire, to keep dogs and wild animals out.

- If you have gaps in your fence such as spaced wood or chain wire and you wish to stop people putting their hands through then I recommend shade cloth secured with shade cloth nails, or wire ties for chain mesh fences.

- To extend the height of your fence the easiest way is to secure star pickets or wooden rails to the existing posts and roll out chain mesh, chicken wire, or plain mesh.

- Another great trick is to run a wire from post to post secured by chicken nails and slide on a plastic downpipe so that when the dog jumps up the pipe spins, not allowing the dog to get a grip.

The Backyard

The pup will be into everything so let's start by checking for all chemicals and dangerous items that can poison the pup. Make certain that all of your chemicals are secured in a closed cabinet on higher shelves. Chemicals also include snail bait, rat baits, weed sprays and bottles, petrol, and cleaning products. Chlorine can also be a risk and puppies can easily fit through a pool fence. It is also a good idea to roll out a layer of shade cloth along the pool fence to avoid the pup's risk of drowning. Sharp tools from saws and drills are also a danger, including nails, screws, and wire, which can blind a puppy. Check around your property including fences and work areas for protruding wire and nails and other sharps that may cause injury. Fish ponds can also be a risk so you may have to place a sheet of mesh over the top and check stairs and patios and other areas where the pup can fall.

Now that we have covered all the stuff that may be a danger to the dog, the next thing to check is anything of value to protect from your puppy. You will find that pups will chew items left around, especially if they have your smell on them, so flip flops, shoes, and socks are prime items to chew up. Place all items of value up high, such as sunglasses, remote controls, etc. Finally there are items in your yard such as air conditioning units, water pumps, and electrical wiring the pup may want to chew. These can be secured by building a mesh or wooden box around the unit or using plastic piping to run electrical cords through. If you always use the same type of toy with your dog, such as plastic or rubber, you will condition your pup to associate these materials with play, so when the dog sniffs out a rubber hose or plastic pipe the dog may start chewing it.

In the House

The pup will be exploring every bit of the house and will figure out all the heavy odour bases of the family. The dog may start going to the toilet in one of the children's bedrooms because of the heavy odour base or in the hallway, as the pup can smell the toilet. If the pup is more dependent on one family member there may be small acts of marking with urine over other family members' odours. The crate training will help the dog to hold off going to the toilet and waiting till it is let outside, and as they do this a few times it will become habit. I will get more into toilet training your puppy in Chapter 4.

Again, inside the house keep all the chemicals stored away and put up high all of your valuable items that can be knocked over and broken. You can also close bedroom doors and condition the dog only to stay in certain areas of the house, such as the lounge room or kitchen. The other advantage of crate training your pup is that it conditions the dog to be calm in the house as well as toilet training it.

Other items to check out are children's toys that may choke the pup, like Lego blocks. In summary, a little bit of hard work here preparing for your new pup may save you great heartache when you get your puppy.

So now you have avoided your new puppy getting poisoned on your chemicals, drowning in your pool, escaping your fenced property, injuring itself with your tools, choking, getting electrocuted, falling of your patio, and getting trapped. Congratulations, your preparation has saved your puppy pain and your heartache and lots of money in vet treatment!

Gaz Jackson

What Dog Equipment Do I Need?

As a professional dog trainer I clearly understand how important it is to have all the right gear at your fingertips. I also demand to have the best available dog gear and if I can't buy what I want I have it custom-made. I only use the best when I'm training and also when I'm on operational work with my dogs. It's not just the leads and collars but also the many other items for you and your dog's comfort. So let's start with some of the basic items you need when you get your pup; then we will go through a list of items that you may need when you start training your dog.

The Basics

1. Two water bowls for the home.
2. Feed bowl.
3. Bedding mat and hammock.
4. Crate for transport or toilet training.
5. Assorted toys (plastic, rubber, wood, rope, etc.).
6. Storage containers for dog gear and food.
7. Car travel kit filled with some of the basics.
8. Dog coats for colder climates.
9. Grooming and bath items from shampoo to brushes.
10. Medical items for prevention of ticks and fleas.
11. Good quality collars and leads.
12. ID tag and microchip for your dog.

Obedience Training

1. Leather collars.
2. Slip collars or lasso.

3. Choke chain (if required).
4. Head collar.
5. Three-foot and six-foot foot leads.
6. Ten-metre-long line.
7. Treat pouch.
8. Clicker.
9. Toy holder or clip-on belt bag.
10. Equipment carry bag.

Obedience Handler

When training it is important that the handler is dressed comfortably with the option of carrying a belt bag with toys, treats, and a clicker. The handler should have all the gear to transport their dog to training locations, such as a dog travel kit.

Tracking, Cadaver, or Search and Rescue Training

1. Long line.
2. Variety of harnesses.
3. Dog vests.
4. Scent items for training.
5. Ground flags for tracklayer.
6. Reflective tape or LED lights for dog.
7. Booties and doggles.
8. Transport cage.
9. Collapsible food and water containers.
10. First aid kit.

Gaz Jackson

Tracking, Cadaver, or Search and Rescue Handler

I highly recommend that if you wish to train your dog for this work then also train yourself. Things you can do include joining a local search and rescue group and completing first aid courses so that at a later stage you will complement your well-trained dog. Become familiar with survival techniques, including reading a compass and using GPS. Another great way to get educated is to join one of the wildlife and bush walking groups. The last thing rescuers want is to waste time looking for you and your dog, so be an asset, not a burden. Get advice from professionals on how to kit yourself out for your local environment.

Detection Dog Training

1. Training and operational vest.
2. Leads, collars, and harness.
3. Canvas scent bags.
4. PVC scent tubes with plugs.
5. Metal scent boxes.
6. Gloves and odour-handling equipment.
7. Magnetic scent caps to stick on to metal walls.
8. PVC scent pods.
9. Scent training boxes with PVC windows.
10. Remote scent box ball thrower.
11. Scent detection room or wall.
12. Specimen containers for target and control odours.
13. Scent safe and carry boxes.
14. Cardboard boxes.
15. Reward toys or food.

Personal Protection Training

1. Heavy duty collars and harnesses.
2. Heavy duty police lead and training leads.
3. Choke chain for collar back-up.
4. Long line.
5. Tie out chains and snaps.
6. Basket muzzle.
7. Training and operational dog vest.
8. Pinch collar (if required).
9. Electric Collar (if required).
10. Secure kennel and travel cage.

Personal Protection Training Handler and Decoy

As a handler of a protection dog it is very important that you have good quality footwear and operational pants or a vest. When you go through the training of getting a dog to bite you are also responsible for protecting the public from your dog. You can start by having a strong dog-proof enclosure and transport cages with signs. Ensure the dog is secured at all times and you have high quality leads and collars doubled up onto a choke-chain. The last thing you need is for an innocent citizen or your decoy getting bitten due to faulty equipment.

Gear the decoy may need during the training of a law enforcement dog may include a full body bite suit; concealed arm pads or sports sleeves; neck, hand, and head protection; whips and rattle sticks; rags; bite tubes; leg bite bars; apron; leather bib; and brace.

The decoy has a very dangerous and important job and it is very hard to find a good one. Most decoys will have their own equipment and will not utilise other people's gear. However, you can have a very talented decoy that does not own a bite suit, so this will limit their talents.

On a recent overseas trip I was unable to take my bite suit so I was given a body bite suit for a training day and ended up black and blue and yellow, with several puncher holes in my arms.

What About Welfare, Local Government, and Regulation Rules?

Animal Management will vary all over the world, from next to no management to very strict rules when it comes to dogs. I can't give you all the answers here, but I will cover some basics that will assist you to understand your responsibilities as a dog owner.

I recommend you contact your local animal management authority to get the list of local laws and information with regards to services provided, such as dog parks. Most authorities will have an annual registration for pet and work dogs and other will have a lifetime registration. When you get your new puppy or adult dog, register all the details, and it is highly recommended to have your dog microchipped. Some authorities make this compulsory and others optional, but many lost dogs have been reunited with their owners due to the microchip.

If your new dog is already microchipped ensure you register the dog in your name, otherwise if your dog is picked up by the pound it may be returned to the previous owner. Some authorities will offer a discount on registration if your dog is obedience trained and others will have a much higher registration for certain breeds such as pit bulls, other aggressive and menacing dogs, and even working dogs.

As an owner it is your responsibility to keep the public safe from your dog so if you have an aggressive dog then you must ensure the dog is kept behind dog-proof fencing or in a dog run. Children can also put their hand in the cage or fenced area and authorities may have a 'safe footpaths policy', which will make you liable if someone gets bitten through your fence. A great idea is to have a panel or wooden fence and if you have an existing chain wire fence you can cover it with shade cloth to stop hands going through. If you need to extend the height of your fence you can attach poles and run chain wire along the top.

Some gates have a hole to put your hand through to unlatch the gate. This is another way a person can get bitten, so make up a small steel basket to place over the hole and latch. Another good idea is to always have your gates padlocked so people cannot just walk in. If a person jumps over your fence and gets bitten however, then they have entered unlawfully and you will have a better chance of not been liable.

When walking an aggressive dog, make sure it is muzzled, or if you walk the dog without a muzzle, choose a quiet route. Signs are another safety idea for protecting the public. I have heard many people over the years refuse to put a sign up saying 'aggressive dog' as it may be an admission of liability. On the other hand, if you have an aggressive dog and don't let the public know about the unseen danger, it may be considered a man trap. Using words such as 'aggressive', 'dangerous dog, 'attack dog', etc. lets the public know of the unseen danger but it can also be an admission and used against you if a person gets bitten. The best way is to warn the public of the unseen danger without admission, so signs such as 'Beware of the Dog' and 'Dog on Patrol' can be seen as a warning that there is a dog on the premises, so be aware. Signs like this inform the public and remind them to close the gate behind them or watch their step as the dog may be asleep on the footpath. For security some people who either have a friendly dog or no dog at all will place up a sign stating that trespassers will be bitten. Other good signs are say things like 'Entry by appointment only and upon own risk', or if you have your place fully secured with dog-proof fences and locks you can use 'Restricted area, dog on patrol, all access strictly prohibited'. When traveling a vehicle sign to use could say 'Security dog in vehicle keep clear'.

If your dog is involved in an attack of a person or animal it can be classified as dangerous and you may have to pay a massive yearly registration and comply with several restrictions. Some of the restrictions can be to always muzzle the dog in public or for the dog to wear a dangerous dog reflective collar or be penned and you must notify authorities if you move or sell you dog. Other dog authorities may refuse to take a dangerous dog in their area and people may not buy your dog if it is attached to a dangerous dog order.

The dog must be exercised so if your dog is penned then you must let the dog out for at least an hour per day and always ensure the dog has access to fresh drinking water. You also must treat any medical condition so the dog is not suffering in any way, and have the dog groomed. You can contact your local animal welfare group to get more information on the care of dogs and other animals.

In summary, have your dog registered and microchipped, in a dog-proof yard with the right signs to protect your dog and the public.

Gaz Jackson

Now I'm Ready for My Ultimate Dog!

Now that I have given you some information to help you get closer to finding your ultimate dog, it is now your job to do your own research as well. Many people in the dog industry are so fanatical about their breed and they believe it's the greatest dog breed in the world and you will be shot down in flames if you try talking about another breed.

I will go into more detail in regards to the breeders in upcoming chapters to assist you in securing the best dog for you. Here is a checklist that you can tick off and see if you are ready for the next step of locating your ultimate dog.

1. I know what I want in my ultimate dog in work duties and as a pet.
2. I know the breed of my next dog and my secondary breed.
3. I know what sex I want.
4. I know if I'm getting a puppy or an adult.
5. I know the costs in purchase and yearly expenses of a dog.
6. I know how to prepare my home for my new dog.
7. I also know the dog equipment I need now and into the future to train and care for my dog.
8. I have spoken to the local dog control and I am updated on the rules and regulations from fences to signs and being a responsible owner.
9. I am satisfied with my choice and I have discussed it with my family and friends.

My ultimate dog breed is_____

Sex_____

I will choose a puppy_____

Adult_____

I will locate my dog from_____

If you already know what you want, congratulations, you are ready to read on to find out where you can get your ultimate dog. If you are still uncertain of what breed you want or anything else, continue reading this book, and also start conducting your own research on the internet and with your local dog control, breeders, and obedience clubs. You may find you will have to see many dogs and talk with the owners before a breed just takes your heart. If breed is not important then you may wish to check out the many pounds and rescue shelters to find a great dog to work with.

Chapter 2

I Choose a Puppy

I am now in Sydney, Australia, sitting on the banks of Sydney Harbour with the Sydney Opera House on my right and the Sydney Harbour Bridge on my left, writing Chapter 2. I am in the middle of a national dog training tour as key speaker for a dog trainers' dinner function.

Introduction to the Puppy Industry

The puppy breeding industry is very big and there are thousands of purebred dog breeders and many more backyard breeders. The industry produces millions of puppies for sale and many end up in pounds or welfare groups for rehoming.

As well as the breeders you have the many dog breed clubs that organise dog shows for their breed. In most cases the committee members and the judges are all long-term established breeders and when they have champion dogs that have won several shows, the dollars roll in for stud fees and puppy sales.

From commanding high stud fees to very expensive puppies for sale and the great publicity for their dogs in the club magazines, it is a very lucrative money-making business for them. Many have quit full-time employment and concentrated on professional breeding, and some run what are no more than puppy farms with dogs living in cruel conditions in a life of breeding, that are then put down when the bitch can breed no more.

There are many high quality professional breeders that will breed high quality dogs in very good conditions, but at the end of the day it's about making money.

Don't believe the well-worn line that the breeder is only breeding to improve the breed; if this was the case the dogs would be sold at cost-price under contract to show and develop and improve the breed.

When breeders advertise to 'selective homes only' it is more than likely that they have a massive waiting list and the price will go up as well. Committee members of dog breed clubs love selling their pups to members of the club, and presto! These dogs win more and the demand gets higher.

The breeders can and do make a lot of money and if you take an example of a popular or rare breed, the pups can sell for thousands of dollars each. If a breeder has five bitches and a stud dog and they sell pups for $1000 each they can produce $30,000 in the first year based on thirty puppies. If they decides to sell fifteen of the female puppies on breeders' terms (reduced price in return for one litter), then in under two years they have another fifteen litters producing approximately $90,000 plus another five litters from their first five bitches. This can give the breeder a potential income of over $150,000 in two years. Remember, this was based on starting with six dogs; many breeders run puppy farms and can have hundreds of dogs. They will run continual advertisements on the internet, selling their pups. In most cases stud fees and puppy sales are 100% cash-only business.

Personally I have bred many litters over the years including Malinois, German shepherd, Rottweiler, poodle, and several other breeds. I have also been actively purchasing puppies on behalf of clients around the world from the backyard breeders through to the big puppy farms, so I have seen a lot. In every case it is puppies for profit, and on the odd occasion a litter is produced to keep a puppy from the owner's pet dog. The breeder will put a high price on the puppies and what they cannot sell they will take to a pet shop or an animal refuge.

I have hundreds of stories from over the years about breeders and dealers—way too many to mention here, but here are a few tricks some breeders may use:

1. When you call a breeder you will be asked a group of questions, like what you want the dog for. Typically, whatever your answer is, their pups will be perfect for you.

2. They will get you to come out to view the pups and the price will go up depending on what car you drive. The price may be $500, and when you arrive in a luxury car the price may be double.

3. The litter is usually divided into three pens; the first pen has the runt of the litter and the second has the rest. When the breeder knows over the phone what sex pup you want then the best one is placed in the third pen. This special pup in the third pen is the one the breeder says they're going to keep because it is one in a million. The runt will sell for $800, the rest $1000, and the special one $2000. You will be surprised how many people will take the third. When the buyer is gone the breeder then places another pup in pen three, who is now the new pick of the litter, selling for $2000.

So now let's go through a list of places you can get your puppy from so you are well informed before you start.

In Chapter 3 I will cover how to test your puppy to ensure you have the best chance of getting a pup with great potential. Then we will go over how to raise your pup into a young adult ready to train.

Gaz Jackson

My Ultimate Puppy from the <u>RSPCA</u> or a <u>Welfare Group</u>

In my career I have known dozens of people that work for the RSPCA, from volunteers to full-time employees including inspectors and kennel staff. I have known some of these people not only on a professional basis but also privately, so I have a very good understanding of operations and the RSPCA's professional and private beliefs. I also know countless people that run welfare groups helping to rehouse dogs and puppies and the foster carers that look after homeless dogs till they have a forever home.

I have the highest respect for these people working in very challenging situations to help dogs that do not have a voice but that are the victims of human greed or abuse. Animal control in many places employ welfare groups to run the kennels and rehouse homeless dogs. There is a continual flow of people surrendering their pets for many different reasons, from moving to a townhouse where they cannot take their dog, to selfish reasons. The animal control are always picking up stray dogs daily, or after a storm or fireworks many runaway dogs are brought into the kennels.

The unfortunate reality is that many dogs are put down due to injury, age, disease, aggression, or just because there are too many dogs in the kennel facility. When dogs come into a welfare organisation to be rehoused the dog is left to settle in for a few days, then is temperament-tested to ensure the dog is safe in the community around other dogs and people. If the dog passes this first test then the dog is booked in to be vaccinated and wormed and de-sexed, ready for rehoming.

Every organisation has different—some very strange—rules and beliefs, so some of them are outlined here.

Collected from the information I have been entrusted with by individuals who have worked for the RSPCA in Queensland Australia, the organisation does not believe in working dogs or any exercise that will put a dog at risk, so many dogs are put down as they do not fit the family pet criteria. What this means is that if a dog has aggression the dog will be put down; often, no dogs are supplied to guard dog trainers even though hundreds of dogs can be rehabilitated and trained as law enforcement dogs. Military is banned, as training a dog to detect explosives will put the dog at risk, yet the dogs suitable for this work are no good as pets and may fail so they too are put down. High-drive dogs that don't pass the evaluation as pets but are suitable as wildlife detection dogs are also put down.

The rules of the RSPCA are different in each country and they are constantly changing; many more dogs can be saved just by relaxing some of these rules.

I am proud to have saved hundreds of dogs from being put down, and staff at the RSPCA have referred many aggressive dogs to me as they knew that if they accepted the dog it would be destroyed. There are many other organisations that care for homeless dogs that run off donations, sponsors, and sales of dogs.

I was speaking with an RSPCA employee who told me that some rescue groups that advertise that they are a 'no-kill' shelter get highly marketable dogs from the RSPCA and advertise them on their site, and what they can't sell they return to the RSPCA to be put down if they cannot be rehomed.

It's so important that regardless of some crazy rules we should all be supporting the RSPCA and other rescue groups in our local areas, by becoming a foster carer or donating money or items to help homeless dogs. The staff at these organisations have a very difficult job and are very caring, empathetic people who love animals. They also need our support, so even if you don't get your dog from here, please support these wonderful people from the RSPCA and other rescue groups. I would also like to give a special mention to the great foster carers of homeless dogs.

You may not be able to get your preferred breed from a welfare group, but if this is not important then my number one recommendation is to search the rescue shelters to save the life of a homeless dog. You will also have a massive choice of pure and cross-breed puppies and adults.

Depending on what you want there is a good chance you may find a highly driven, suitable dog, but also consider this: many of the dogs that come into a rescue organisation have been abused and may be hand-shy, scared of people, or un-socialised, which may render them unable to be groomed into your ultimate dog.

In a kennel environment the dog may be timid or unsure and pass all the tests for rehoming, yet when the dog gets to your home it becomes a totally different dog. I have seen many dogs that pass the RSPCA test and after they settle into their new home they end up as aggressive dogs that are very territorial. The reason for this is that they may have been abused or un-socialised, so then when they go to such a loving family the dog's confidence skyrockets and they become very protective. Due to the lack of socialisation the dog's suspicion is already high.

In summary, contact your local dog rescue group or animal control department and speak to the staff and view some of the dogs available. You may not get your next dog from there, but it will give you some great education on dog ownership and the opportunity to speak to some canine care heroes.

My Ultimate Puppy from a <u>Pet Store</u>

There are many pet stores that sell puppies in the windows of their store. Some may only have a couple for sale and others have dozens of pups for sale at any given time. There are now specialist puppy stores that only deal with puppies of several breeds.

When you go to the pet store you may see some happy, healthy pups playing in the window in a clean, well-maintained pen, and some people fall in love on the spot and impulse-buy a puppy and then buy from the store everything else you need to care for your new dog. It sound great, doesn't it?

Well, here is the reality of a lot of the pet stores selling puppies, which I have seen first-hand. Pet stores purchase their dogs from a list of backyard breeders that produce little cross- and pure-bred designer dogs. The RSPCA bust so many puppy farms with dozens and in some cases hundreds of dogs in terrible conditions used solely for breeding and supply of pet shops.

I recently went on a bust with the RSPCA and dog authority to a puppy farm and I was horrified to see over fifty dogs on chains, locked in small cages in bad conditions. I witnessed slaughtered cows used to feed the dogs and pallets of stale bread and yogurt and buckets of filthy water everywhere. The condition of the dogs made me sick, and after all the dogs were taken from this puppy farmer many were put down due to their poor health while the others went through months of rehabilitation to be rehomed. This person supplied several pet stores.

I know of many other puppy farmers and all of them supply pet stores. I also know several other backyard breeders who have several toy dogs that have spent most of their life pregnant or mothering pups. When the pups are old enough they are all put in a crate and taken to the local pet store where the owner is paid between \$250 and \$800 for each animal.

I have a very strong view of pet stores selling puppies and that is that we should boycott the business completely. Do not ever purchase a puppy from a pet store or you will be a part of the problem and supporting puppy farms.

There are groups like Oscar's Law that are actively trying to stop puppy farms and pet stores from selling puppies. Debra Tranter, the founder of Oscar's Law, has worked tirelessly to make a difference and with her efforts has saved thousands of dogs from puppy farms and cruel living conditions. Here is Oscar's story and details of how you can help or donate to this great cause. The world needs more people like Debra.

Oscar's Story

Oscar was rescued from appalling conditions at a puppy farm in central Victoria, Australia.

Oscar suffered terribly and had infected ears, dental disease, and inflamed, infected gums. His fur was so matted it felt like concrete, and his skin was barely visible. Once his matted fur was shaved under general anaesthetic due to the pain he was in, his skin was covered in abscesses caused by grass seeds.

Oscar's freedom was short-lived. Days after his rescue, authorities seized Oscar and returned him to the puppy farm.

Oscar is alive and is back home once again after enduring five years on two puppy farms.

For the last eighteen months a team of dedicated people have worked tirelessly to gain Oscar's freedom. Oscar is finally receiving the care and love he deserves and is learning to live life as a dog rather than a breeding machine in a factory.

There are thousands more dogs like Oscar suffering on puppy factories across Australia that need your help. One of the most powerful ways you can help dogs like Oscar is to raise awareness. Please take the time to email your state political leaders; you may wish to add your own personalised comments to the pre-written letters.

The power is in our hands with every choice we make as consumers. Never purchase puppies from pet shops or online trading websites. Instead, choose from your local animal shelter, pound or rescue group—these puppies or adult dogs will all be de-sexed, microchipped, and ready for a happy life with you.

Empower and educate everyone you know about the truth behind the pet shop window and glossy websites. Together we can shut down this industry that views our best friends as primary producers.

We need your help to get justice for Oscar and other dogs like him who are factory farmed in Australia. We need all of you to spend five minutes a day to lobby both the Liberal and Labour parties and call for the abolition of puppy factories. We want Oscar's Law. The current legislation is not working.

Oscar's Law

- Abolish the mass production of dogs. Make factory farming of dogs illegal.
- Ban the sale of factory farmed companion animals from pet shops, online, and in print media.
- Encourage people to adopt animals from shelters, pounds, and rescue organisations.
- Westpac Oscar's Law Inc.
  BSB: 033372 Acct: 421050

Gaz Jackson

- Email info@oscarslaw.org
  Website oscarslaw.org
  Debra Tranter 0417 536 539
  debratranter@gmail.com
- Tell the government to commence running a REAL campaign about true and responsible pet ownership.
- Go to oscarslaw.org to find out how you can be part of the solution and help us shut down puppy factories.

My Ultimate Puppy from the <u>Internet</u> or <u>Paper Classifieds</u>

Over the years I have purchased hundreds of dogs from the newspapers and internet for the sole purpose of training in obedience and protection and to resell as highly trained dogs. These are of course adult dogs I am buying, however I have purchased several puppies on behalf of clients from around the world. You will come across the backyard breeders, puppy farms, and many families that may be breeding a single litter with their family pet. The advantage of the classifieds and internet is that you will know of all the litters on the ground at the moment in your local or expanded areas.

The internet and classifieds are great resources to start your search with, and here are some key questions you can ask over the phone so you can decide if it is worth you viewing the puppies.

1. Are you a registered or professional breeder?
2. Is this a one-off litter or do you breed regularly?
3. Is this a repeat mating?
4. Have the parents been breed surveyed or titled?
5. Have the parents been hip and elbow x-rayed?
6. Are the puppies from working or show lines?
7. Have the pups been microchipped, vaccinated, and wormed?
8. Do you have any health defect guarantees?
9. Can I do a heap of tests on the pups?
10. Does the pup come with pedigree papers and a medical certificate?

These are a few questions that will let the breeder know that you know what you're doing. I will go into more detail later in this chapter in the checklist. Now you have all of this information you now know if you're dealing with a professional or a puppy farmer or a one-off breeder, and whether or not you should go out and have a look at the litter.

I can also recommend that you go out and have a look at several litters so you can get more information on the breed and talk to several breeders. This will allow you to compile a heap of information and to compare different litters. You may be very happy with one litter you see, but then see another litter that is so much better than the first. It is so important that you are educated so you can make the right decision the first time.

I have seen so many people over the years who have impulse-purchased a puppy from a pet store, only to realise that the pup is totally wrong for their lifestyle. In most cases you cannot take the puppy back, or you will develop a strong bond and therefore keep the puppy.

My Ultimate Puppy from a <u>Backyard Breeder</u>

I will take a moment to clarify what a backyard breeder is; in many cases it has been used as a derogatory term by professional breeders and animal control officers who describe them as amateurs. Backyard breeders describe themselves just as breeders. So what is the difference between a professional breeder and a backyard breeder if they are both breeding puppies at the household? Well, the only difference is that the professional breeder may produce more litters but is registered to canine control council and is a member of a breed club.

Apart from this the backyard and professional breeder may have the exact same setup breeding from home. The backyard breeder is anybody who whelped a litter of puppies from their home; this could be an accidental litter or a planned litter from their pet. If this person buys several dogs for the purpose of breeding and selling puppies they are still a backyard breeder, but are on the borderline of becoming a puppy farmer.

In some cases the backyard breeder is not set up with all the professional whelping and breeding equipment. The pups may be whelped in the laundry or garage then advertised in the classifieds or on the internet when they turn five weeks of age. The puppies are advertised at this age to provide the breeder with the best chance of selling all the puppies at eight weeks of age. The backyard breeders that produce cross-bred dogs for hunting in some cases end up giving the pups away or taking the unsold litter to a welfare group for rehoming.

Over the years of purchasing many puppies from backyard breeders I have found that most are excellent people who genuinely love their dogs and do the right thing. I have also seen some horrific people with no empathy for their dogs, who see them as just a money-making source. Ask the right questions on the phone and you could find your ultimate dog from a backyard breeder— and if you're not worried about pedigree papers, you will also save a lot of money.

If you show up at the breeder's house and the dogs are in poor condition or you believe they are living in a bad environment, it is your duty to report the breeder to the relevant authority. I also recommend that you do not support in any way the puppy farms by purchasing dogs from them or from pet shops.

My Ultimate Puppy from a <u>Registered Show</u> <u>Breeder</u>

I have spent several years meeting show breeders of many different breeds of dogs, and it is always an experience to meet a show breeder. I found that a lot of breeders are so obsessed with their breeding that they can talk for hours about how good their dogs are. They are also very quick to slander every other breeder and detail how another breeder's dogs are inferior to their dogs. You will hear everything, from corrupt dog judges to any other stories the breeder wishes to tell you about. The most common reason why people get out of the show and breeding scene is because of all the backstabbing, slander, and bitchiness.

Not all breeders fit into this category, but I have seen many that do, and it's important that you don't get involved in breeders' rants and raves. That being said, breeders are in it to make money. Period. When you contact a breed club you will get some recommendations of select breeders, but not all, and it is difficult to try to sift through all the club competition to get facts.

My recommendation is to speak with several breeders, from the club officials to the club members, to work out who is producing the highest quality puppies. Research online as well as get a list of the breed standards and photos of high quality dogs of the breed of your choice.

It is also a good idea to join the breed club to get the latest show dates and info on breeding. With all this information you are a step closer to choosing your top breeders. You may also have information on breeders internationally as well as other breeders who are local or nationally-based. There may be huge costs in importing a puppy, as well as the fact that you are buying blind, and due to quarantine requirements the pup may miss out on the critical period of development due to age restrictions. Then you have to work out, do you book yourself a return flight to check out the breeder and bring the puppy back with you?

In conclusion, you do not go to a show dog breeder if you want a working dog, unless the breeder does produce the characteristics you require, such as crazy ball drive, etc. There may be a big difference in quality based on location from local breeders to countrywide. If you are buying from a show breeder then ensure you have in writing the guarantees of the breeder, including pedigree papers. If the breeder cannot offer them to you on the spot then don't leave until you have a declaration from the breeder in writing that you will receive papers. I have lost count of how many times puppies were purchased by my clients from breeders and they never received the papers.

My Ultimate Puppy from a <u>Registered</u> <u>Working Dog Breeder</u>

I have had a lot to do with working dog breeders over the years and they are a breed of their own. The breeders are always trying to produce the fastest, hardest, most rock-solid, highly driven working dog. The working dog breeders spend so much time on their breeding programs, often importing schutzhund (German protection dogs) or dogs from police or IPO, or even semen from world champion dogs. These breeders are the ones that usually supply many law enforcement agencies and are only interested in seeing their dogs in working roles.

Military and many large canine units have their own breeding programs and most if not all are full of working dogs from the proven performers.

There are many working dog clubs that produce high quality working dogs and supply the dogs to breeders, etc. All of these groups go hand-in-hand with a united endgame of producing or working with a strong, highly driven working dog.

Talent scouts from law enforcement agencies are checking out working dog clubs and the breeders that produce these highly driven animals. The breeders that produce more dogs for law enforcement are the working dog breeders and this is my choice for places to start looking for your ultimate dog.

To track down some working dog breeders, start with your basic internet and classifieds search to start with a list; but remember, they are all self-promoting their business and their breeding so it's all going to sound wonderful. You will also see many of their past glories in their promotions, but that won't help you if they only have an average litter at the time. The next step is to contact your local dog squad, government or private, in the police force, prisons, or military to see if you can have a talk to the head trainer. The next step is to contact your local schutzhund clubs and talk to the trainers there. Ask about who is producing your top working dogs and you may get a couple of leads on proven working dog breeders. With this extra information you should have a list of top breeders you can then do some research on, including when their next litter is due. You will be able to narrow your research down to one breeder, then have your name down for a future puppy.

My Ultimate Puppy from a <u>Dog Training Centre</u>

Firstly, I have to say that I ran a dog training centre for thirty years, and I also know many other operators, so I have a very in-depth knowledge of what happens in these centres. Dog training centres are usually a kennel complex purchased to board dogs whilst the owner is on vacation. As the operator tries to increase the income of the centre during the off-season times of the year they will usually venture into other areas. These will include doggy day care, pet shop and food supplies, dog training programs, dogs for sale, and of course, puppy breeding. In a lot of centres I have seen the adults are in kennels in the boarding facility and their only purpose in life is to produce pups to raise the owner's income. This kind of setup is another form of a puppy farm—just within a commercial kennel complex.

You may have show and working dog breeders who purchase a dog kennel to expand their operation, or the breeding may just be a small part of an existing business. Many of the operators of dog training businesses buy in dogs for sale and they will also secure breeding females and wait till she comes in session to get a litter to on-sell. I found that of the many trainers I have dealt with, a large majority just want to produce the pups to sell, then sell the mother and father. Many will be just buying in females of any breed, then either use a boarding dog of a client to mate or they have their own stud dog. Unless a dog training centre has been breeding for some time, don't get your dog there unless you are after something average.

I have bred many different types of dogs over the years, from cross-bred toys to working German shepherd and Malinois dogs.

I have also had several one-off litters from many other breeds. The bottom line is that we bred them, raised them to eight weeks of age, then sold the litter off. We then gave the mother away to a good home in return for one litter within eighteen months. So an investment of $500 for the mother was turned into two litters that returned over $5000.

There are also a few training centres that have extensive breeding programs and may produce many years' worth of high quality puppies as this is a big part of their business. You may be able to get your ultimate dog from a dog training centre, but do your research first!

Checklist and Questions for the Seller

Once you have done all your research on the breeders, covering from show to working dogs and training centres, you should be able to shortlist a final group of breeders. You know what you want your ultimate dog to do and how it should look. You know what sex you want and you know you want to get a puppy. You have done the research on the many different types of breeders and now it's narrowed down to one type of breeder, and you have located the top three breeders that may have your ultimate dog.

The first point of contact is the telephone to get more information from the breeder and to find out if the breeder knows what they're talking about. I know that as a trainer and breeder I get numerous calls every day and potential clients just rave on about their dog and insignificant information. A lot of the time I have had to say, 'I can't help you.' The reason for this is that if I spoke in detail to every person, I would never get off the phone.

My tip is to call and introduce yourself to a breeder and say you are interested in purchasing one of their puppies. Offer to call back at a convenient time that will suit the breeder. The reason for this is that every day breeders are running around feeding pups, moving dogs, training, etc. Offer to send the breeder through a list of questions by email following the phone call. When you have established a call-back time, have your list of questions handy, but don't design an interrogation for the breeder. Many times in the past I have had puppies for sale and someone will ring up and either be rude, arrogant, or very demanding. When this happens I say, 'I'm sorry, I have nothing available at the moment, please go elsewhere.'

When you speak to the breeder, always be polite and respectful, and also be careful of how much you tell the breeder what you want the dog for—chances are that whatever you want, their dog can do it. Start off by asking general questions and it's best to take advantage of their ego first.

For example you might say, 'Good morning, I have been highly recommended to buy my next puppy from you as you are one of the best breeders that produce excellent quality pups.' You will be so surprised as to how a breeder will open up after you appeal to their ego. The breeder will normally ask you a few questions such as whether you have owned a dog before and what the dog is for (e.g. as a pet or to train).

Explain to the breeder that you are looking for a high quality dog that you can raise to be a part of the family. Maybe you are also wanting to do some training at a later stage, and what are their dogs like to train with? Please note that there are breeders that are totally against training dogs for guard work and may refuse to sell you a pup for training. Ask the breeder if it's okay to run through a small list of questions you wrote down so you won't forget. Remember: don't interrogate the breeder, or they may not sell you a pup.

Start off with a general question, such as, 'Can you tell me about your breeding program, and what do you think of this current litter you have?' This will get you a heap of info on the parents' breeding and why this is such a great litter. After you have this then start asking more specific questions. If you have too many questions over the phone you may not get the chance to even view the pups. This is when the breeder takes your name and either files it in the trash or puts you at the back of the list and hopes all the pups sell before they get to you.

If the breeder has a litter available then the phone call is to get good information for you to take it to the next step of viewing the puppies where many more questions can be asked.

Here are some more general questions you can ask via email or phone or in person.

It is best you get some of your answers via email in case you need them later for legal action against the breeder or to send the responses back to the breeder if there ends up being a disagreement. Email questions to ask:

1. What age can I view the puppies and what age can I take the pup home?
2. Have the parents been breed surveyed and temperament tested as being suitable for breeding?
3. What titles if any do the parents have?
4. Do the puppies come with pedigree papers and are they restricted or on breeder's terms?
5. Will the pup have up-to-date vaccinations and be microchipped?
6. What guarantees do the puppies have in regards to genetic faults such as hip and elbow dysplasia?

The biggest complaints I have seen over the years targeting breeders from people I know and myself is that the pup is supposed to have papers and they never arrive. The breeder is chased up for months and all the buyer gets is many excuses, such as that it was lost in the mail or that the breeder sent the paperwork in weeks ago, and eventually the buyer gives up. In every case the breeder tells the buyer by phone that the dog has papers so that there is no physical record at all for legal action.

The other big complaint is that the pup turns out to be a genetic mess and is put down as a young adult. I have not seen any successful case from a buyer against a breeder in this situation; most just cut their losses and walk away. One breeder I spoke to said that when a buyer rings him up to say his pup has hip dysplasia, he tells them to get the x-ray and mail it to him so he can show his vet. When he receives the x-ray confirming the problem, he tells them to take the dog to the vet and put it down and send him the certificate and he will replace the pup. In every case the buyer could not do this as they fell in love with the pup.

I have been successful in getting a full refund or exchange from a breeder due to my position in the dog industry. When I purchase on behalf of a client I firstly have the emailed answers so I have a record. In the event of a client calling me to say the dog has medical problems, I ask for proof, then I ask the breeder for a full refund. I also send back the copy of the agreement via email with the consumer national law extract that states 'if a product is faulty the buyer is entitled to exchange, repair or refund'.

When you speak to the breeder on the phone you can ask many general questions about the litter and the breeding, breed characteristics, and faults. Questions should range from diet and exercise to how much socialisation the pups are getting.

Ask if you can come out to view the pups when they are around four to five weeks of age. The reason for this is you can check out the breeder's operation and see if the pups meet your criteria. The other reason is that you may be able to pick your puppy on the spot and leave a deposit. If you wait till the pups are eight weeks of age, you may find you arrive and most are already sold, and how mad would you be if you see your ultimate pup in the litter and you can't buy it?

If you cannot make up your mind when the pups are five weeks of age you may be able to pick the top two to four pups and ask to come back in a week to do more tests. You can also ask the breeder to monitor the behaviour of the pups for the most motivated or dominant puppy or the one with the highest food or chasing drive. This info along with your own tests will bring you closer to choosing your ultimate dog. If you do pick a puppy early then get a photos so you can identify the pup when you pick it up. Other ways to identify the pup is to fit it with a collar or use nail polish on the toe nails.

This now brings us to conducting tests on a litter of puppies to choose the best puppy.

Chapter 3

Puppy Tests

I am sitting in a donga, which is a converted shipping container, in a mining camp on Groote Eylandt in the Northern Territory. I have been out this morning training environmental detection dogs, then in a fishing boat with a successful catch of queenfish and one shark that was thrown back.

***

With all the research you have done, you now have chosen your breed and checked out a few breeders. Now you have selected the breeder and a litter is available, and you also know what sex you want. This is now the exciting part where you get to pick your puppy from the litter.

The litter may be of eight puppies of four males and four females, or perhaps of only three puppies of two females and one male. You may have to pick between several puppies or only two; do you just concentrate on the sex you want, or the entire litter and grade them all, picking the top two or three? Then there is the health of the pups and any faults that you can or cannot live with or that may affect the working life of the dog. Looks is another thing that may be very important to you, and there may be one odd pup that is double the size of the rest of the litter. These are all factors to consider when trying to choose a puppy in a litter.

Then there is also the behaviour of the pups and how they respond to stimuli. Some can be dull with no motivation, and others may be high energy, chasing everything. Some will be independent and others super responsive to stimuli. In most cases it is so hard to get a puppy without compromise, and if you wait for the perfect type of pup you may never find one. In other cases you may be lucky to get the genetic base you want with health, colour, drive, and everything else fitting to what you want. There may be only a handful of local breeders and you may be forced to fly in a puppy without seeing it first, which is very risky.

When sourcing a puppy, I don't just show up when the pups are eight weeks of age only to find out the litter is poor quality or are sick-looking or that most of the litter is sold. I will always ask if I can see the pups at around four to five weeks of age. This gives me a chance to speak with the breeder and check out the care they have for the pups and their knowledge of the breed. It's also a chance to see if they are a puppy farmer, who I refuse to buy puppies from. If everything looks good, then I start checking out the litter and the parents. In most cases the breeder may use a stud dog, so the father may not be available to view.

On my first contact with the breeder in person I will ask for all the paperwork on the litter, which can include the parents' pedigree papers and breed survey details, and ask whether they are aware of any health problems in the breeding. I will also ask for all the medical certificates so I know that the pups are vaccinated and checked for or on treatment for internal parasites. A trick I have used with great success in the past is to ask the breeder on the phone if they would mind if I bring with me a veterinary surgeon friend of mine to check out the pups and ask some questions. The same works when I tell clients that have been told all this great stuff about a highly trained adult dog for sale, and they ask if they can bring Gaz Jackson with them.

When I see the litter, I firstly check out the hygiene and how the pups are cared for by the breeder. I have seen some high-breed litters and the breeder has destroyed the pups' confidence by kicking pups out of the way or hitting the pups with the food bowl. Puppies that have been through traumatic experiences under eight weeks of age will be unsure of people or hand-shy; this is not what you want as your foundation for training.

Things I'll look for on the pups are fleas and ticks, rashes or crusted skin, or if the pup is covered with faeces. I will listen to the breathing for coughing, sneezing, or vomiting, and any discharge from the eyes, ears, or nose. I check if they have diarrhoea and if they are skinny or pot-bellied. They may be dehydrated, so just pinch the skin and it should pop back if the pup is well-hydrated. Next, I will look to see if they are lethargic or just have no energy.

If the pups in the litter have some of these problems then it may be a good idea for 'thanks but no thanks'. If you feel the breeder is a puppy farmer or the dogs are in inhumane conditions, then report the breeder immediately. If you are unsure, then you can always pay to have a local veterinary surgeon check them out.

If everything adds up and the breeder is great and the litter looks fantastic, then it is time to move to the next stage.

You are limited with tests you can do on a litter of pups that are four weeks of age but it is a great chance to check out how they interact with each other and their mother. In nearly every case when I have checked out a litter early, the pups are feeding or sleeping. I ask the breeder if the pups can be removed from the mother and placed in another area such as a grassed yard. This gives me a chance to check out how active they are in a new area; do they all just huddle together and whinge, or do they start using their noses and crawling aimlessly, exploring the new area?

I will place my finger on a bit of meat and hold it in front of a pup and start to see what interest the pup has in trying to get to it or not. I will also start using a squeaky toy or a whistle to see the reactions to the sound; they may be curious and even crawl towards the sound, or just tilt the head, or have absolutely no reaction at all. I will then throw a brightly coloured toy a few feet from the pups to see the interest or whether the pups show avoidance.

Another toy I use is a sock on a string, and this really gets them going.

Ultimately, the first visit to a litter is to establish a meet-and-greet with the breeder and check out the condition of the pups. Observe interaction and play to see if they are confident or dull and what kind of drives they have to play or for toys and food. You will also be able to narrow down your choice of pups to the top three, or even down to one puppy.

If you at this stage have picked your puppy on the first visit, ask the breeder if you can place a hold on that puppy. Most breeders will be happy to do that with a deposit.

It's a good idea to bring a little collar to place on the puppy and take a lot of photos. If they all look the same, then bright pink nail polish on the nails can also help. Ensure you have a written receipt with details of your chosen puppy that is signed by the breeder.

I will contact the breeder via email and call on a weekly basis to check up on the welfare of the pups and to finally organise a date to come back to pick up the pup.

If you haven't chosen your pup and wish to come back when they are eight weeks of age, you may find they are sold out or that most have deposits on them. Also, if you are a pain to the breeder, they may just say that there are no pups available for you. Personally as a breeder I have done this several times in the past—the client just had to be rude or demand totally unreasonable requests, and that client went to the bottom of the list.

If you do get a chance to test out a litter of pups at around seven to eight weeks of age, here are some tips to assist you in this process.

As you are looking for your ultimate dog, you will be looking at the potential the puppy has for you to train it. For example, you may need a high energy dog with strong prey drive to chase toys, and high food drive. A high energy dog with the correct genetic base and high drives will be much easier to train. You may have the correct genetic base, but the dog has no motivation and is arrogant or dull, making it hard to train, and you will consistently be motivating the dog.

You may not be looking for a high energy dog as you want a calm and relaxed dog that is totally chilled out and will just be a great family pet. The biggest mistake I see over and over again is the family going to a top of the range working dog breeder to buy the best, or else they go for the wrong breed such as a Belgian Malinois. This mismatch will give the family a dog that doesn't stop and has so much energy and can be a nightmare to live with. Other mismatches occur when families go for the looks, not knowing too much about the breed traits, and end up with a dog that's arrogant, too high energy, or that has high aggression.

Many puppy tests are based on a points system or the puppies are graded by colour to categorise each puppy. For example, green may indicate a social-safe pup, yellow may indicate a high energy and excitable pup, and red may indicate fear or aggression. These systems work well in pound situations where a lot of dogs and staff are involved. Law enforcement agencies also have their own systems for evaluation of puppies and adults.

As you are just trying to find a puppy for yourself, I prefer to do a collection of tests to check trainability of that dog. You may find the pup passes with flying colours in some tests and fails in others; then you have to deduce the training potential and whether you can achieve your ultimate dog with this eight-week-old pup.

So, a quick shopping checklist:

1. You are happy with the breed and sex you chose.
2. You did your research on the different lines of dogs.
3. You did your research on the breeders.
4. You have found the right breeder and breeding program and, finally, a litter that is available.
5. You checked out the litter at four to six weeks of age and they are all healthy, with the correct paperwork.
6. You know what you want in your ultimate dog.
7. You have already planned your puppy raising and training programs.
8. You are now ready to pick and take home your ultimate dog.

Now let's get started; whatever tests you do with the pups, you can grade them into four categories and you can give them a score within each category. Later, for adult dogs, we will use a complete Psychological Profile Chart and the tests will vary in accordance with the purpose of the dog. Different organisations call the puppy tests 'temperament tests', but temperament + environment = behaviour, so this means we are checking out the genetic base plus environmental factors. The pup may be totally genetically sound but abused by the breeder, causing a strong fear that is environmental. If the pup has a strong fear, regardless of what caused it this may render the pup totally unsuitable for your purposes.

The four categories that all the tests will fit into are:

1. Positive response to stimuli.
2. Fear or nervous response to stimuli.

3. Aggressive response to stimuli.
4. Focus intensity and recovery timeframe.

The classification within each of these categories will be up to you, from extremely responsive to no response at all, so you might like to put together your chart to grade the pup's response on a a scale of one to ten; or using colours like green, yellow, and red; or using levels like high, medium, and low.

The classifications I like to use within each of the categories are:

1. Extreme
2. High
3. Medium
4. Low
5. None

Some pups will have multiple reactions to a test, so I will give an example and outline how this would read on a chart.

Test and Chart Example

You roll a basketball near the puppy. The pup reacts with strong focus, then chases the basketball until it gets two feet from it. Then it stops, its tail goes down, and it turns and shows indecision, then it turns and barks at the ball. After a couple of seconds the pup stops and stares at the ball for thirty seconds then walks off, forgetting about the ball, to play with the other pups.

Positive response to stimuli: High / Focus: Average
Fear or nervous response to stimuli: Low / Focus: Low

Aggressive response to stimuli: Medium / Focus: High

Focus intensity and recovery timeframe: Focus: High / Recovery: Slow

I would like to point out that fast recoveries are excellent and slow ones in adult dogs is an indication of no socialisation or that the dog has been through a traumatic experience. Puppies that have strong fear at eight weeks of age are going to affect your training program with fear or dependency-related problems.

You may find only some of the tests are applicable, such as food motivation tests. The fear and aggressive response may not be applicable as the dog shows zero response to fear and aggression during the food tests, so the result may be:

Food test (test details here)
Positive response: Low
Focus: None
Fear response: N/A
Aggression response: N/A
Recovery time: N/A

So in this case the pup shows a low response to food motivation; is this because the pups were just fed by the breeder or the pup was in sleeping mode, or does the pup just have no motivation for food? Other variables you need to consider are things like extreme temperatures or uncomfortable walking surfaces that will affect the pup's motivation.

These are just some of the variables that you need to consider, and by the time you have finished your tests you will have a good profile on your potential ultimate dog and whether the pup will make the grade.

I find the best time to do the tests is mid-morning or mid-afternoon when the pups are most active, and ask the breeder not to feed the pups before you get there if in the morning, or a few hours before if in the afternoon. You may end up with passed out pups that you have to wake up to try to do the tests.

You can also add notes to each test after you have graded the pup, for example: "The pup was relaxed totally whilst being handled but showed stress and nervousness when the feet were touched, but recovered very quickly."

I also want you to pay particular attention to pups that have a fear of and slow recovery to tests due to being oversensitive. Fear is a natural reaction and the pup should recover quickly, but if the pup cowers then does not recover and remains fearful of the item or the tester, it is an indication of oversensitivity and the pup most likely will not be suitable.

Touch, Smell, Sound, and Visual Stimuli Tests

First watch the entire litter and how they interact with each other to get an idea of energy levels and rank within the pack. You may also see the most dominant pup and the runt of the litter.

1. Pick a puppy up and pat the pup all over from head to toe including ears, tail, and feet.
2. Place puppy gently on its back and lightly place hand on chest.
3. Place puppy on its own in a grassed yard away from the mother and litter and observe if pup plays and explores, sits and cries, or tries to get back to the litter.
4. Squeeze gently the pup's ear or toes between your thumb and finger to cause minor discomfort to test sensitivity and recovery.
5. Place a collar and lead on pup to test reaction.
6. Slowly take the pup for a walk, pulling gently on the lead.
7. Place some food a few feet in front of pup, then hold pup back with a hand on its shoulders.
8. Have someone hold pup on ground, show pup some food, and walk twenty feet away; pup is then released.
9. Rub food on ground about ten feet downwind from the pup.
10. Place plastic tub of food with lid on and holes punched in it down in front of entire litter.

11. Place bone down for the litter.
12. Place food in bowl in front of pup then put your hand in whilst the pup is eating.
13. Take bowl away when pup is in the middle of eating.
14. Place tasty treat on a chair or similar object so that treat is just out of reach of the puppy.
15. Blow a whistle with two short blows followed by several quick blows a minute later.
16. With your own voice, speak in high pitches to the pups then lower your voice to a deeper sound.
17. Make three claps of your hand, then call the pups.
18. Shine a torch or LED light around the pups.
19. Show them a shiny object like a beach ball or reflective mirror.
20. Use a squeaky toy and throw it near the pups.
21. Tie a sock on a string and drag it around.
22. Put food in the sock and drag it around.
23. Test possession level and intensity when the pup is playing with a toy or food.
24. Place food and toys in basket to test interest.
25. Return all the pups to the mother and enjoy.

When you have done all of these tests or some of them you will have a much better idea of if your puppy will make the grade. The more active and the more motivation the pup has to food and toys, the easier it will be to train. If the pup has great focus this is also a bonus.

If you do these tests and find the pup is scared of many things and has slow recovery or sits down and has little motivation, then this pup will not be suitable unless you want a simple, relaxed pet.

You will also see highly strung and dominant hard character pups that may be stubborn and can also be a pain to live with and train.

To sum up, there is no guarantee that you will get your ultimate dog from a puppy you choose, however with all your research on the right breeding program, getting the right litter, and selecting the right puppy, your chances are very high. Now it's up to you to raise this pup and train it into your ultimate dog.

Chapter 4

Raising Your Puppy to a Young Adult

I am sitting in a 100-year-old steam ship in Queenstown, New Zealand, with an elderly lady playing a piano in the lounge area. I'm looking out at the beautiful snowcapped mountains. I have just driven the beautiful Arthur's Pass yesterday after a successful dog training seminar tour.

***

I think all of us have heard horror stories of disobedient dogs that chew up everything, bark at nothing, show aggression to dogs and people, jump on guests—and the list goes on.

Most of these problems are directly related to how the dog was raised as a puppy, and if raised right, you may get the perfect pet. If you are raising a working dog such as a Belgian Malinois for detection or bite work, then the dog will have incredible amounts of drive and energy and will be very hard to live with. You will also be developing the drive in preparation for the dog's working life. There are, however, some things you can do to make life a little easier living with a working dog, and I'll get to that soon.

When the dog's behaviour is broken down into three parts it is so easy to understand why your dog does what it does.

Temperament + Environment = Behaviour

The dog is born with a genetic base that cannot be changed, which includes the breed characteristics, and you will have variations within the breed. For example, you have dogs from working bloodlines that are strong in character with massive chasing or prey drives and pain tolerance that may be very suited to training.

The soft character dogs have a lower pain tolerance and generally environmental factors affect them much more.

This is why so much is focused on top breeding programs for law enforcement dogs; these breeders produce highly driven, hard character dogs with great potential to become police or detection dogs.

As another example, border collies in general are used to herd sheep and not cattle; they have great drives but do not have a strong defence and pain tolerance. This is why cattle dogs are perfect for the job of cattle herding.

You can also choose a mismatched dog for your lifestyle such as a strong character, highly driven German shepherd, and you only have a small yard and you are away most days of the week. The result may be terrible; the better choice would be selecting a breeder that breeds German shepherds for the family market that may be softer and less driven.

Environmentally, dogs can be given hundreds of problems and you will get different behaviours in accordance with their genetic base and breed characteristics.

Let's first look at how to raise your pup, then, what will be some of your dog's most likely behaviours when exposed to good and bad stimuli.

Do not take your puppy home from the breeder before eight weeks of age as the pup needs this time to socialise with the littermates. Dependency, separation anxiety, and overprotectiveness later in the dog's life can all be caused by taking the pup too early from the litter or too late from the litter. Having the pup sleep in the bedroom is another way of developing a dependent dog. Lack of socialisation during the critical period of development will also cause many problems. Stress and anxiety related behavioural problems such as chewing and barking are also dramas you have to deal with if you get it wrong with the raising of your pup.

The most important time in your dog's life is called the critical period; the reason it is called the critical period is because it is *critical*. Do not underestimate the importance of this time in a puppy's life. The critical period can be divided up into five stages and each stage has a name and a timeframe. There are always arguments about the exact day of transition to the next stage and about when the critical stages finish. I don't want to get into this argument, so let's just say that from birth to sixteen weeks of age is really important. I will break it down to give you an understanding of the timeframes of the five stages and the different behaviours that may develop as a result of different scenarios.

Stage 1

The pups don't open their eyes and ears till around ten days of age. Some may be earlier, others later. So the senses the puppies have are thermal, touch, and smell. The pups will all group together to gather warmth from the littermates and the mother. When the pups are suckling their mother, their noses are pressed against her belly, breathing in the strong odour of the mother's body smells. This, over the next few weeks, will create an association of the mother's smell with food. So the two big associations for the pup are body contact with the litter for warmth, and smell of the mother with food.

Stage 2

In the second stage of the critical development is when the eyes and ears open, at around ten to fourteen days for the eyes and approximately thirteen to seventeen days for the ears. The pups will be starting to move about and become aware of their surroundings. This is when they start to develop really quickly, with wagging their tail, crawling around more actively, growling, etc.

Stage 3

The third stage is after three weeks of age when the pups will be moving about a bit more and starting to have play fights with the littermates, and it's about the time they will start on solid foods. Human interaction is also good during this period, achieved by holding them or placing them in a grassed yard for thirty minutes or so.

Stage 4 and Stage 5

In the next couple of weeks the pups will be exploring, playing, and discovering many sounds, smells, and sights. In the past it was recommended that the pup stay with the mother until seven weeks of age, and then it was seven weeks and four days, but the accepted timeframe for the pup to come home now is eight weeks of age.

Gaz Jackson

Problems with Taking the Puppy from the Litter either Too Early or Too Late

Now let's have a look at what happens when a puppy is taken away from the mother either too early or too late.

If a puppy is taken from the litter, as an example, at four or five weeks of age, then you can expect many behavioural problems as the dog gets older. At the age of four to five weeks the puppy is still very dependent on the mother and the littermates by having consistent body contact with them. The puppy now has a very clear association of the mother's body odour with food so this becomes a pacifier for the puppy. When the pup is in contact with the other pups and smelling the mother's odour the puppy is totally content. This is why when you take a four-week-old puppy from the litter and place it in the yard on its own, most will yap and struggle to try to get back to the litter, so the pup will not settle. When you place two puppies in the yard, they may settle due to the body contact, then still try to get back to the litter.

What this means is that the pups are still very dependent on the mother and littermates, so if a puppy is taken at that age from the litter the dependency will immediately transfer to the new owner. By the time the pup reaches eight weeks of age the pup is already very dependent on the human, and this will develop more severely over the next few months and, more than likely, the life of the dog.

If the dog is taken at the correct age of eight weeks and then spends every hour of the day with the owner then that dog will develop a strong dependency and find it hard to be on its own. The fastest way to create a dependency problem is to have the new puppy sleep in the bedroom with you. I cannot stress enough how dependent this will make your dog.

The other side effect of the dog sleeping in the bedroom is that now you may have changed the rank structure. If you have children and you have the dog sleep in the bedroom, in the dog's mind it is now number three in rank over the children as you have created a pack within a pack. When the dog believes it is higher up in rank over some humans, there are some things the dog may do to establish its leadership. It will go from doing nothing at all, to being arrogant to the children, ignoring them, or standing in-between you and your kids. Other acts can be urinating in the children's bedroom or rolling on the children's items to place their odour on top. In more severe cases dogs will display dominant body language over the child with the tail and eye contact and even growl. In the worst cases children are bitten or have been killed by the family pet all because of incorrect rank structure and dependency.

This is also why when you pat one dog the other dependent one pushes in or growls at the other dog. If you have one dog that is allowed in the house and the other one is not allowed, then when you let the dog outside the other dog may aggress it or enact small acts of dominance.

The next common way for the dog to become dependent on the owner is if the dog has a terrible experience concerning a person or another dog, making the dog a bit paranoid when it comes to the outside world. It is so important that from eight weeks of age the dog gets heaps of socialisation and has good experiences. Try to avoid any traumatic experiences occurring for the dog in this early period.

I have seen many dogs that through no fault of the owner have been exposed to a traumatic experience and it has affected the dog for years after.

The most common one is the puppy of eighteen weeks of age is taken to the off-lead dog park and is beaten up by a large dog and injured. As a result, the dog may be scared of all other dogs, or just large dogs, or just male dogs, or just black dogs—depending on what the pup associated with the experience. The result will be that when you take the dog for a walk, the dog will be sniffing worriedly for other dogs and its anxiety will be high. The dog's ability to learn will drop as the dog is under stress waiting for another dog attack. When the dog sees another dog it may try to hide behind the handler as the traumatic experience will develop dependency or the dog may puff its hair up defensively, growl, and even try to attack the other dog.

Other traumatic experiences can be from humans or cars so the dog may react badly to raised arms, objects in a human's hands, or even car noises.

The next common way your dog could become dependent is that during the critical period of socialisation, which is between when you got the puppy at eight weeks of age and sixteen weeks of age, the dog has absolutely no socialisation and only sees the family and the inside of the fenced yard. The dog rarely sees people or other animals and its entire world is in the yard. The result of no socialisation in this critical stage is, again, that the dog becomes dependent on the owner and is paranoid of the outside world and develops high suspicion. The dog will bark at anything that moves, from a strange noise to the neighbours' talking. The dog then becomes very territorial so there is continual marking of the fence-line, and when the dog sees a stranger it may display fear-based aggression. The unsocialised dog is afraid of everything, but over time the dog may respond to conditioning.

Here is a list of conditions that creates a dog that is dependent, experiences separation anxiety, or is overprotective.

1. Puppy taken from mother and littermates too early e.g. at four or five weeks of age.

2. Puppy always with the owner 24/7, or 100% of the time the owner is home.
3. Puppy sleeps in the bedroom with the owner.
4. Puppy has a traumatic experience.
5. Puppy is unsocialised in the critical period before sixteen weeks of age.
6. Puppy remains with its mother and littermates for longer than twelve weeks.

If your dog has any one of the above problems, there is a great chance the dog will end up dependent and the severity will be in accordance with the dog's genetic base; for example, strong character dogs have higher stress levels and are more independent than softer character dogs. Other dogs may have several of the above problems, such as being taken from the litter at four weeks of age, having had a traumatic experience, sleeps in the owner's bedroom, is with the owner twenty-four hours a day, or is totally unsocialised. In this case the dog may end up as a basket case. When the dog is away from the owner, the dog will go into a total meltdown, shaking, panting, pacing, and howling until the owner returns.

So here are some lists of things that happen with dependent dogs. Not all dependent dogs will have every problem, but they all will have some of them. Dependency then creates separation anxiety in the overprotective.

Dependency Problems

1. Sticking their nose in your armpit, groin, or bum all the time.
2. Chronic licking of your skin and mouth to gather odour.

3. Jumping to lick you on the mouth.
4. Will only sleep within your scent pool, within a few feet of you.
5. Follows you everywhere.
6. Tries to have constant body contact with you.
7. Takes any item with your odour on it such as bras, underpants, etc.

Separation Anxiety Problems

1. Pacing at fence-line for your return.
2. Panting—quick and shallow pants caused by stress.
3. Chewing items up that have your smell on them.
4. Anxious chewing of furniture.
5. Howling or barking at nothing to relieve stress.
6. Sitting in the blazing hot sun or freezing cold, waiting for the owner.
7. Listening intently to cars blocks away for the sound of your car.
8. Digging a hole and laying in it on the fence-line.
9. Chewing itself up.

Overprotective Problems

1. Aggression from behind fence at all dogs and people.
2. Dog stands between you and any other person.
3. Marking another person or property.
4. Becoming agitated, with hair standing up on back when people approach.
5. Showing aggression or launching an attack on people or dogs that get too close to owner.

There are several more problems that may be associated with a dependent dog, so you can see now how dependency may affect your dog for life. This will affect the training and your lifestyle with your pet, so the bottom line is that the early weeks form the most important period in your dog's life; get this right, and you are well on the way to having the ultimate dog.

In twelve months of doing private lessons around three countries, here is the number one reason I discovered for dogs becoming animal or human aggressive, dependent, and nuisance barkers. The answer is: *veterinary surgeons.*

Now think about this for a moment.

Here is the explanation: the first professional the new puppy owner deals with in most cases is their local vet. In so many cases the owner has been advised by the vet or vet nurse to keep the dog away and not to socialise the dog until it has all the vaccinations and checks, which in many cases occurs after the critical period. This advice is consistent with so many vets. So here is the typical chain of events:

1. Vet tells owner to keep pup away till all the needles are completed.
2. Owner keeps pup in backyard until around four to five months of age.
3. Pup becomes dependent, develops separation anxiety, and is overprotective.
4. Pup matures, barks at everything, cannot be walked as is too aggressive.
5. Vet suggests to get the dog de-sexed and you do.
6. Problem still bad so the vet puts your dog on medication.
7. You put up with the problems for the life of the dog, or rehome the dog.

Puppy pre-schools are great but many are run by vets in the same place where they treat sick dogs with parvo and CANINE cough and other diseases. The class is run by the vet nurse, and it's a great opportunity for the surgery to get clients for life and promote their services and pet food supplies.

In conclusion to this subject on vets, it would be better for them to tell all their clients to heavily socialise their pups in the critical period of development, but to avoid high risk areas like dog parks and kennels.

How to Fix Dependency Problems

1. Place your dog in a boarding kennel for ten days in isolation. The dog will stress out and may go off its food, but it will adapt. The dog will be conditioned to spend long periods of time on its own.
2. Bring dog back home and keep it in the yard and out of the bedroom.
3. If the dog can see you from outside, place it on a tie out for some time each day so there is no contact with you.
4. Put the water away from the back door in another spot, away from the house.
5. Feed the dog at random times and at different spots each day.
6. Place a smelly shirt belonging to the owner on the dog's bed outside.

Do this for around ten days, then you can relax it a little; however if you have the same routine as you once did, when you bring the dog back from the kennels, then dependency will be the same after a couple of days.

It's amazing the things that can happen with your new dog during this critical time in the dog's life; you can have the most highly bred dog and still end up with a dud due to environmental factors.

Now let's look at how you can develop your dog after getting it from the litter at eight weeks of age, and how to do it right. I will also cover some other exercises you can do in accordance with what you want for your ultimate dog. For example, raising suspicion and developing a dog for guard or law enforcement work is different from developing a dog for a pet or as a detection dog.

Take your puppy from the litter at eight weeks of age and immediately start the socialisation with everything you can think of without scaring the puppy or giving it a bad experience. A great start is to book into a local puppy preschool; they do a great job, it's heaps of fun, and you will learn a lot from the very talented vet nurses. Just be aware that this may be a high risk area for disease.

Dog parks are also great, but be very careful that the pup does not get rolled by a bigger dog. Pups that have had a bad experience with another dog will usually develop animal aggression or submission to new dogs. A dog park is also another high risk area for disease.

Animal aggression is directly caused by lack of socialisation or a bad experience from another dog, so this is why it is so important you have a social animal by the time it is six months of age. If you have an animal aggressive dog I recommend you see a professional dog trainer for evaluation and socialisation in a controlled environment.

The pup should see heaps of people and be fearless of all, so the more people who come to your home the better, and you can also get friends to take your pup down to the park. At home, get your pup used to spending time on its own. Condition it to stay in the garage or outside overnight, not in the bedroom.

When you bring your pup into the house it will be overexcited and very active and may go to the toilet on the carpet, so I recommend you invest in a dog transport cage or cat cage for the pup. Place the cage in a high traffic area of the house such as between the kitchen and lounge, place the pup in the cage for around one hour, then put it outside again. This will achieve two things: the first is that the puppy is forced to remain calm in the house as it can only stand or lay down while watching the family. The second is that the pup will be less likely to go to the toilet in a confined area, especially if it is taken outside a few times a day.

Another tip to help the pup learn to pee outside is for the owner to pee in the area you want the pup to go to. Female owners can pee in a cup and transfer it to the designated area. The pup will learn very quickly that this is the toilet area and you will get fast results. When you are outside with your pup and it goes to the toilet, repeat a word to it such as 'toily' or 'pid' and after some time you will be able to say the word to your dog and it will go outside to the toilet on command.

If your pup is exposed to bad stimuli, this may affect it for life; now let's look at examples and consider the possible outcomes.

A strong character dog that is unsocialised may develop into a fearful biter and is a danger to people and animals. As this dog matures and becomes more confident its aggression levels will increase to a strong, defensive aggression. Some of the body language the dog will show will be raised hair on the base of the back, and extremely fearful dogs will have raised hair from the shoulders down to the base of the tail. This dog will have an aggressive bark and ears flattened against its head. As this dog is scared of the outside world, its confidence is highest in its own property, with the owner inside and the security blanket of a fence in front of it.

A soft character dog may react with submission and be more likely to be dependent on the owner.

One thing you should never do to any dog is to hit it with your hand or an object as a punishment. When the owner does this they will usually yell at the dog as well. As the dog associates pain with the raised voice, the dog will become vocally dominated and react with submission when any person raises their voice. You will end up with a cowering dog that is scared of you and other people.

By the time your pup is six months old it should have been heavily socialised to people, dogs and other animals, and traffic. It should also be comfortable spending time on its own, so you should end up with a social and safe dog in the community. By taking the puppy with you in the car you can visit many places to expose it to the views and smell of that environment. The beach is a great location to take the puppy, or a crowded marketplace or sports match—but don't overdo it. You can start off with the pup in the car watching and smelling the new environments. Having toys and food to change the puppy's focus can also help a great deal. You can also give people food treats to give to your puppy so that the association with people is great pleasure.

You will need to walk the dog on a lead, so here are some tips: when you first place your puppy on a lead, have it on a flat collar. Do not use a choke chain, and do it at home. Condition the puppy with a collar first, then put the lead on it in your back yard. Let the puppy pick up the lead and drag it around a little. Next is to have food treats to change the focus, then you can hold the lead and walk around with the puppy. If you place a lead on the pup for the first time then drag the puppy, trying to get it to walk, then the association will remain negative and the first reaction will be avoidance behaviour.

At this stage we are not trying to teach the puppy any obedience at all, just that the lead is fun and associated with praise and treats. When this is achieved you can have control of your puppy in different environments, from the park bench on a busy street to the beach. You know you did it right when you go to pick up the lead at home and the pup gets excited because it associates this with positive things.

By the time the puppy is six months of age the socialisation should have exposed the pup to everything it may see in its life. So as a checklist: heaps of people, smells, work environments, traffic, dogs, and farm animals. Walk through the forest, beach, parks, and town to expose the puppy to everything, including noises.

Conditioning the Pup to Love Obedience

Now the pup is conditioned to the lead and associates that with happy experiences, but what about doing obedience training with the pup?

I will start to condition the pup to commands from eight weeks of age but I will use absolutely no force at all and I will make it fun, with food and praise. I will keep the state of training conditioning less than one minute long, but the repetition will last for months as a fun game and the pup will learn at its own pace.

At eight weeks of age I will use small, soft meat treats and hold them just above the pup's head and say 'sit' a few times; if the bum goes down as the dog is looking up then I immediately give the pup the treat and praise with 'good boy/girl'. Don't be in a hurry with this one as it may take two days or two weeks, but once the pup creates the association with sitting for a treat then you are on your way.

For 'heel' I will do this off-lead with a puppy by walking, holding a treat to my side around the height of under my left knee. As the pup walks to try to get the treat I'm repeating the command 'heel' in a happy voice and 'good boy/girl', so again the pup is learning without knowing. I will also give the pup the treat, then have another one so the pup learns to walk beside me and gets treats along the way.

I would also like to point out, don't do overkill on the obedience at an early age—I have seen many puppies and young dogs wrecked because the owner did so much repetition and raised voice correction that the pup hated the obedience and worked through fear. What the handler has done in this situation is diminish the dog's drive and confidence before it has even developed. I have seen many dogs that were then unable to complete training in detection and protection due to lack of confidence and diminished development totally caused by the handler. Don't make this mistake.

Many police departments do so much work on obedience first that this then overrides other exercises from the handler, placing the dog in a 'stay' situation a lot of the time; for example, the dog may be so obedient that the handler gets beaten up and the dog won't move (because it has not been commanded to) in case it gets in trouble. Then there is the detection dog that does the behaviour of searching as an obedience command, but is looking for nothing; or the dog just cowers when the handler gets close. In all these cases, obedience can override the dog's other functions, so go easy.

When I train detection dogs I do absolutely no obedience at all and just develop a dog 100% focused on getting the target odour. When this is done then I will slowly do the obedience training separate from the detection and then bring both together. This is also the case in training personal protection dogs, as I will do the protection first to get great confidence and drive with the bite work, then do the obedience separately before I bring the two areas of training together.

Develop the dog's drives first, before anything else in adult dogs—but in pups, only use positive training and associations and build drives before any form of enforcement is used. The foundation of socialisation and positive training in the pup will develop a great attitude, and this is the foundation for all your future training. Remember: Temperament + Environment = Behaviour.

You can do a first-class job developing a pup from eight weeks of age, but if the genetic base is wrong for what you want you will get a dud. Some people get lucky and get such an awesome genetic base in their dog that they can make a heap of mistakes and still end up with a great dog.

So if you have a great genetic base, you got your pup at eight weeks of age, and you have socialised the dog heavily, then this is a great foundation for every type of training. The first thing I suggest is to start conditioning the young dog to the future worksite, so if you are going to train your dog as a narcotics detection dog for employment on the docks, then start getting it out to smell all the odours of the docks, go on ships, etc. If it's search and rescue you want to train for, then expose the dog to the natural environment.

Agility is also another good skill to condition the dog for on different surfaces, and I always found that the children's playground is the best to start off on. Stairs, buildings, elevators, travellators, and carparks are all great for conditioning too.

Please don't underestimate the importance of socialisation and the conditioning process as many dogs have been rendered useless for their speciality work as a direct result of this even though they may be excellent in that field. Here are some examples.

1. A search and rescue or environmental dog that is animal aggressive and would rather chase an animal than look for target odour.
2. A protection dog that won't bite a decoy due to fears such as stairs, a raised arm, loud noises, etc.
3. An area protection dog that is useless when someone has food.

There are many more examples and there are many more conditioning exercises that you can do to help prepare your dog for its working life. With the above examples they may all have been avoided in some of the following ways:

For example 1, the handlers socialised the dog heavily to animals and the environment and used correction if the dog showed any interest in other animals.

For example 2, the dog was conditioned early in life to objects and hands raised above the dog's head. This will help in protection training with the decoy. Running up and down stairs and exposure to loud environments as a pup would also have made a big difference, so neglect in conditioning back then could mean being assaulted due to the dog's failure now.

In example 3 the handler could have bait-proofed the dog, made the dog sit and wait for the food until the command was given, and used treats in stranger avoidance training.

A very important step in getting to your ultimate dog is the development of natural drives so that as a trainer you have something to work with. At this stage if you have a dog with a great genetic base and you heavily socialised the pup during the critical period and conditioned the young adult to future working environments, then you are on the right track. Development of drive does not just start at six months of age; this is a process that is started at eight weeks of age or earlier and continues throughout the dog's life. Back in 2001, to prove this I got a Malinois puppy obsessed with a sock on the end of a stick, and with the use of frustration this pup went crazy trying to get the item. I then associated the sock with the target odour of marijuana and by the time the pup was eleven weeks of age the pup was doing off-lead drug searches with an active indication, becoming the youngest detection dog ever. The videos of this are on my YouTube channel at https://www.youtube.com/user/garymnk9/videos.

Let's look at some suggested exercises for a future guard or law enforcement dog, and a detection dog or search and rescue dog. We will also consider that the dogs have the right genetic base for the job, are well socialised, and conditioned for future work.

The family home protection dog should be heavily socialised till around six to eight months of age; then, at this point, break all socialisation in the household. What this will mean is that over a few months the dog's suspicion levels will rise towards strangers behind the fence. When the dog barks from behind the fence, give an excited 'watch' command followed by 'good boy/girl'. In the early stages the dog may come back to you or just wag its tail at you, then refocus on the threat. You will find in only a few short weeks that the dog will start to become reliable behind the fence, being a good home alert dog; but the dog is only as good as its suspicion levels at the time.

To raise its suspicion levels, you may need to hire a professional dog trainer to stalk the dog from behind the fence at a distance. When the dog locks on eye contact to the decoy, then the decoy crouches and returns heavy eye contact. This will be considered by the dog as a threat, and the first reaction may be ears forward, a puff of the lips, a small growl, or barking and running towards the fence. The very moment any of these things happen, the decoy spins around and runs away behind a car. The dog will figure out that it has won, so we have raised not only the suspicion but also the confidence.

This can be repeated only one more time and that's it, no more. The decoy then disappears, so no hanging around talking to the handler in front of the dog. After only one or two of these sessions the dog may become more reliable behind the fence and, in combination with praise from the handler, the dog may only need one to three sessions.

Developing a law enforcement dog for doing street work will include, in the training program, bite work on a body bite suit and concealed arms and basket muzzle. The dog can be developed much earlier so the foundation is strong with high suspicion and strong focus. An important part to remember here is don't agitate your own dog, unless it's just a game. The first time the dog sees a decoy it should feel threatened. If you have an inexperienced decoy or agitate a dog when it's too young then the dog will not be threatened and will have no suspicion towards the decoy. You may end up with an equipment-happy puppy that will only chase an arm pad and never bite for real.

In the early stages of development you can play rag games with your puppy and develop its bite through playing with a rag in tug-o-war, letting puppy win. Ball games are also important to develop a strong prey drive and chase. This will also improve focus in training for things like obedience. With a young dog of around ten months you can get your partner to handle the pup on a lead and you can stir the puppy up with a rag. The pup should feel absolutely no threat but should be excited to chase and bite the rag as a game. When the pup is biting the rag you can create a small fight, placing your hand over its eyes, etc. and letting it win. When the pup's drive develops it will be able to run off-lead to bite the rag. You can also place the pup behind a chain wire fence or screen door and stir it up with the rag. The frustration works so well with this scenario, with the pup's intensity raising, and you will get even more barking.

To give you an example of how powerful frustration is: in protection I have had many dogs in kennels that when you test them and start training them in protection they are very average, with low drive; they may bark but with no intensity. The handler will place the dog in a kennel with four other dogs in other kennels.

The decoy would run in and agitate the dogs and within minutes the average dog becomes very intense with the frustration of being behind the fence and the excitement of the other dogs barking. After a couple of sessions of developing confidence and drive behind the fence, the dog is brought out on-lead again and the intensity has tripled.

At this point the young adult should be able to run and grip a tube or rag and fight for it with excitement and win. When the dog sees a ball or rag you should see an intense focus and drive to get it. I recommend that when the dog first sees the decoy it is about fourteen months of age and the decoy wears no protective gear to avoid the pup becoming equipment-happy. The dog should feel threatened by the decoy and as a result the dog will respond in an aggressive, serious, and defensive manner and win. The decoy should not ever back the dog down as this will destroy its confidence; they should only be enough of a threat that the dog is agitated but wins.

The decoy can also use the frustration of being behind the fence as a tool, which will also give the dog a security blanket. Praise from the handler and distance from the decoy also helps. This is why you need an experienced decoy; if the threat is not there the dog will see it as a game or become equipment-happy, and if the decoy is too threatening then the dog will show avoidance behaviour and lose confidence. When the decoy does it right, the dog should show serious aggression towards the decoy, and when the dog gets its first bite it should be able to go straight onto the body bite suit for leg or arm bites.

In detection work there are many average dogs out there and you really need a dog that is OCD about a toy or has extremely high drive for food treats. It's not good enough just to have a dog that chases the ball—yes, it may love the ball, but that's not good enough. A trainer may view over fifty dogs to get the right dog with the perfect drive to start as a detection dog. If you have raised your dog for the specific purpose of a detection dog then the development of drive begins at eight weeks of age. This is the type of drive you need for a detection dog: the dog must be ball-mad—you throw the ball a hundred times and the dog is still going to keep getting it, with little loss of enthusiasm. If you throw the ball in the bushes, the dog should be searching non-stop till it gets the ball without encouragement, even if it takes twenty minutes.

If the ball is left with the dog it will spend its day carrying it around and dropping it at your feet to throw it again. If you place the ball on the other side of a wire fence you want the dog digging, barking, and putting paws through the fence, but not leaving. The same should occur if you put the ball in a tree that the dog cannot reach. The necessity for this drive is so you can carry out long searches without having to worry about motivating the dog all the time. Even after a big day when the dog is tired, you can still do more searches. This drive is developed environmentally and also from the dog's genetic base and breed characteristics.

So here are some exercises to help develop drive in your dog. When you first get your puppy at around eight weeks, after it has settled in you can start by playing games with it using, for example, a tennis ball on a string. You can encourage the pup to play and fight for the ball with retrieval and other actions. When you have finished the game, put the ball away until next time.

Another good game can be to place the dog behind a screen door and tease the dog with the ball from several feet away. I will then bounce the ball off the screen door, and by this stage the pup should be losing its mind with excitement. This frustration will quickly develop the dog's obsessive desire to get the ball.

I will also deprive the dog of the ball for a few days, then get it out and do the same exercise against the screen door. Then I place the ball in front of the door; the dog will be so frustrated that it will be pulling on the door to try to get its beloved ball.

The ball goes away, then I do another session like this the next day; in this case I have used only frustration and the dog is now totally obsessed with getting the ball. Another tip is that if you know what detection you will be teaching your dog in, such as narcotics, then place the ball in a bag sealed with the target odour to start off the association with the narcotic smell.

Another exercise you can do to help prepare your dog for detection training, is have the dog do a passive sit when it finds the target odour. Command the dog to sit, then say a reward word such as 'yes' and throw the ball at the same time. This will link the two associations. Then at a later stage you can have a clean ball in your pocket and when the dog finds the target odour of your other ball in the target odour, you can say 'sit' and bounce the ball in front of the dog. The dog will pick this up quickly. Then you will see the dog actively searching to find the target odour and sit without any command from you. I will stop it here, as one of my future books will go deeper into detection training.

In conclusion, you will need a combination of a strong genetic base, breed characteristics, heavy socialisation, development of drive, and training to develop your ultimate dog. If any one of the above is missing then it will affect your end result.

Chapter 5

I Choose an Adult

I am sitting on a park bench at Point Lookout on North Stradbroke Island on a beautiful sunny day, looking over the ocean, writing Chapter 5. I am here to work on my book and visit the famous koala detection dog Maya and speak with local ecologists.

Introduction to the Adult Dog Industry

The industry is a metropolis of professionals, weekend warriors, and keen amateurs all training, breeding, showing, and competing with hundreds of different breeds of dogs. All of these are competing for the sale of pups, the champion of the next show, or training and selling adult dogs. From pet owners, to greedy puppy farmers, to obsessed show dog people, to the huge egos of dog trainers. On the fringes are the welfare organisations, vets, animal control officers, pet shops, and pet food suppliers. There is a massive amount of people in the dog industry and everyone in their own mind is an expert, has the greatest breed, the hardest dog, etc. So when you sift through all the layers of advice from all these different people you will find that you will be more confused than before.

There are some wonderful, experienced, good people in the industry that have made a career in breeding or training, but I want you to be forearmed so you don't get ripped off or become tied up in people's stories. In nearly every case the breeders and the dealers of dogs are salesman giving you this wonderful story of how grand their breeding is and that this, sir, is the ultimate dog.

I will go through several types of organisations, breeders, and trainers so you know how to deal with them and some of the tricks or policies they use and how you can be prepared and take control.

Gaz Jackson

My Ultimate Dog from the <u>RSPCA</u> or a <u>Welfare Group</u>

I have secured many great dogs from welfare organisations including Maya the koala scat detection dog, Chance the cancer detection dog, Migaloo the archaeology detection dog, Snowy the water dragon detection dog, Archie the koala detection dog, Rusty the cane toad detection dog, and many others used in detection of explosives and drugs and for search and rescue. I have also secured many great purebred and cross-bred dogs for law enforcement training that were sold to military, prisons, and police.

Many organisations are working hard to get dogs into new homes and some have a zero-kill policy while others evaluate the dog to ensure that it is medically okay and within the policy guidelines for age, etc. before making it available for sale.

The process for a welfare organisation to have a dog available for sale is along the lines outlined below, but will vary in different groups and countries.

1. Dog is surrendered to pound due to behavioural problems, owners have to move, or any other reason, including finding out from the vet the dog has a bad medical condition. Some dogs are picked up as strays, so there are many reasons dogs end up in the pound.

2. The dog is given a few days to settle in so a behavioural assessment and medical check can be done. If the dog is outside the criteria, such as having skin problems, aggression, or is just old, they may go straight to death row to be put to sleep.

3. If the dog is a purebred then they may call that breed's rescue group that only rehomes dogs of a certain breed. Other rescue groups may do their shopping for rescue dogs at the RSPCA and only take the marketable dogs. I was disappointed to learn first-hand that some dog rescue groups promote the fact that they are a no-kill shelter but that dogs they cannot get into a home are taken back to the RSPCA to be put down.

4. The dog goes through the behavioural assessment. These tests vary from very basic to very in-depth. One of the basic tests is to use a false arm and place it into the dog bowl when the dog is eating; any aggression is a fail. The testers will check for sociability and also animal aggression. If the dog is an escape artist, non-stop barker, or has OCD fixation on an object, these can all be fails.

5. The dog is then booked with a vet that will de-sex, worm, and vaccinate the dog and conduct many other health checks. The dog then goes back into the kennels until the stitches are removed.

6. The dog, if a stray, is given a name from the staff, bathed, and put in the rehoming section for the public to view. Most take photos of the dog with a description and it is posted online and in the local newspapers.

7. The most popular dogs such as Maltese, pugs, and crosses go very quickly. Other dogs may be put up for sale and nobody wants them so the dog may be placed into a foster care home. Other dogs get into a home and the behavioural problems are so bad

that they can be returned several times. Staff may not tell you this, but they just hope the dog will be good this time and never come back.

8. Once a dog is chosen you will have to fill out paperwork and answer questions with regards to yard size, etc. and your experience as a pet owner. The staff member will give you advice and take you to their shop to sell you dog gear, from bedding, to bowls and pet food. The staff will encourage you to only use positive motivation training, and not to use, e.g., a choke chain. This is in line with their organisation's views.

The following will give you an insight into some of the rules different organisations have. It's important to know these as you may tell them you want a dog for training, which might be against their policies.

1. No dog is to be used as a working dog in detection or protection.
2. No dog is to be sold to a commercial dog trainer or breeder.
3. No dog is to be sold to the military or police.
4. No dog is to be sold for export.
5. No dog is to be sold to apartments or properties without fences.
6. No dog is to be sold to commercial premises.
7. No dog is to be sold as a hunting dog.

Remember, you are an applicant and the staff will be assessing you to see if you are suitable, so if you walk in and say you want a big angry dog to guard your car yard you will be shown the door straight away. The criteria is usually that the applicant must have a secure, dog-proof yard and require the dog as a family pet.

Many dogs are put down for no other reason than their own policies; for example there may be a high quality German shepherd that was brought in due to aggression. Because the organisation does not agree with guard dog training or many other working dog training, this dog is put down. I have first-hand knowledge of dozens of dogs that have been destroyed because of a group's rules dictating 'no dog trainers'.

Many of these dogs easily could have been trained and placed into a loving home or sold as a law enforcement dog. Dogs that have high drive or OCD for a toy are also put down even though many dog units would take them in a heartbeat.

When you walk into a large kennel complex with dozens of dogs barking, it can sometimes be a little overwhelming with the noise and smell. You will see some happy dogs and some very timid, hiding at the back of their cages. Dogs will also be different in a kennel environment than on their own property. On the dog's own property its confidence levels are high and the dog may be very territorial over the owner and yard so it may run to the fence with high aggression, barking at people.

This same dog in a kennel may be scared and intimidated by other dogs, so the reaction to you may be submissive. The number one thing to look for is a happy, friendly, confident dog that has the looks to match. Many people will see their ultimate dog in looks, but the dog may be a terrified mess with limited training potential. Other people find the most amazing personality and drive in a pound dog but it looks nothing like what they wanted. In both of these cases you have to decide if you want looks, personality, or both. I will go through some tests you can do with a dog you have found later, in Chapter 6.

When a dog has been locked up all day it is going to go crazy when the staff let it out on a lead. The dog will see the staff member as the feeder and the freedom person is the one that lets it out of the cage. The dog will more than likely jump all over you with excitement, but don't judge the dog on this just yet. You want to see the dog outside the cage, so get the staff member to walk the dog to the exercise yard, taking note of how the dog reacts to all the dogs it passes. In the yard, let the dog run around for a few minutes so it can go to the toilet and check out the area. From here you can go in to interact with the dog and bring in some food and toys. You will be able to get a good idea of the dog's drive and retrieval and food motivation in the first few minutes, as well as its personality. If you can ask if you can spend half-an-hour with it so you can see what it is like when all the excitement is gone. Most welfare groups will be happy to put the dog on trial, but they still may require full payment up front. I recommend a fourteen-day trial so you can get to know the dog better and also gives it a chance to settle in. In this time you can also do a lot of training and testing.

Questions to ask the staff:

1. Can I see the behavioural assessment or speak to the staff that performed it?
2. Find out as much history as possible, for example, is the dog a stray or dropped in and why?
3. How long have you had the dog for?
4. Has the dog been around cats or other animals?
5. Has the dog had any training?
6. What are the fears the dog has?
7. What is it like in kennel?
8. Can I come back to spend more time with it?

9. What is your return policy?
10. Is there any other info or paperwork you have on this dog from the last owner?

The last question is very important, as if you find out the name of the vet the dog last saw you can contact them and say you're looking at the dog. You can ask if they can pass your number onto the previous owners to call you. In the past I have found out so much info on a dog from the past owner that the current owner does not know or won't tell you; things like the dog being much older than you're being told, or that it has many medical problems, or may have terrible behaviour problems, etc.

Gaz Jackson

My Ultimate Dog from the <u>Internet</u> or <u>Paper Classifieds</u>

The internet is the number one platform people use to sell dogs. Years ago paper classifieds were the best option, and although they are still being used people are flocking to the internet to sell dogs. I have seen the increase of dogs for sale advertised on social media and in buy-and-sell groups. It is very easy for the seller to reach a wide audience; but this method can also attract many conmen.

The dogs available online will cover the entire dog industry, from puppy farmers to professional trainers, dealers, welfare groups, and people selling their own pets. RSPCA and councils will monitor dogs for sale from potential puppy farmers and people who breach the council laws. It is common for puppy farmers and dealers to have several phone numbers and advertise the dogs from other addresses. When dealing with dogs for sale via internet or classifieds, firstly establish what type of person you are dealing with—are they from a professional kennel or training centre or are they a dealer or family that has to sell their pet?

I have purchased thousands of adult dogs over the years from the classifieds and internet and I found the best way is to not beat about the bush. Ask them something like this: 'Hi, I'm calling about the dog you have advertised for sale, can you tell me a bit about him?' From here most will establish that it's a pet and they are moving, or that the dog is becoming aggressive, etc. This will allow you to establish that it is a private sale. If the seller knows their dog has medical or bad behavioural problems, most will not freely let you know.

If at this point you don't get the information you need, ask the seller straight out, 'Why are you selling the dog?' or 'Are you a private seller, breeder, trainer, or dealer?' Most will let you know so you then know what you're dealing with. The next question I ask is, 'Can you tell me a bit more about your dog?' You might want to check if it is a good watchdog or if it has had any training. Is it timid or overly excited? The next question is, 'How is the dog health-wise?' Are all its vaccinations up to date, and check if he has any medical problems or old injuries. You will be surprised how much info you can get just with these questions and in some cases you open the floodgates of info. So from here you now know who the seller is—private or dealer, etc., what the personality of the dog is like, medical history, if the dog has had training, and why it is for sale. This information will determine if the dog is now worth viewing. On many occasions in the past I have spoken to the seller, got the address, and told them I would be there soon, only to find out someone bought the dog before I got there.

Some sellers may be desperate to sell and others that have very popular breeds can put a high price on the dog and still sell it ten times over. I always let the seller know I will have a look at it and if it is what I'm looking for I'll take it on the spot. I also ask if anyone else is coming out to look at it. I have had sellers in the past that use the application method; they will ask everybody to view the dog and take their details and at the end of the day call the successful applicant to come back.

To protect yourself when dealing with dogs for sale over the internet, get as much information as possible from the seller, such as:

1. Ask for cell phone, address, etc.
2. Ask for an email so you can send a couple of questions.

3. When viewing the dog ask the seller to hold the dog so you can get a photo.
4. Most sellers will only take cash and in the past I have been ripped off by the seller taking several large deposits and then disappearing with the dog. If asked for a cash deposit ask for identification of the seller such as a driver's licence.
5. I know of many dogs that disappear only days after purchase and the buyer thinks the dog jumped the fence and escaped. The scam is that the seller sells the dog and gets your address for the receipt. They will ask you whether you're there all day or do you work, etc. and two days later they come around and steal the dog back and either re-sell it or take it back home to its real address. Best is to give a postal address or a relative's address.
6. Find out if the dog is microchipped and papered and if the dog is then the seller has to transfer all the details into your name. On many occasions I have purchased a dog with pedigree papers and the papers never show up weeks later; the seller has excuses, but the usual reality is that they never sent them in. The best way here is to say to the seller that if they can fill in seller's details and sign, then you can take care of the rest. This will protect you from giving the seller your address for the pedigree papers or microchip transfer.
7. Transfer the microchip details immediately because if the dog does escape the animal control authority will contact the seller to say they have the dog.

I have given you some examples of the scams and dishonesty that can occur, but this only occurs a minority of the time. Most of the industry will do the right thing but it is important that you are aware of this to protect yourself. I have purchased so many great dogs from the internet and newspapers and I have also been a victim. Also remember that some people have to regretfully sell their family pet and they are very emotional, so they are looking for the best home, not the first to pull out the cash.

Gaz Jackson

My Ultimate Dog from a <u>Breeder</u>

As you know by now, there are many types of breeders, such as the puppy farmers, professional show breeders, working dog breeders, and amateur breeders who may just be producing a one-off litter. There are a number of reasons that a breeder will be selling an adult dog. For a breeder perhaps one of their past puppy buyers has to sell their dog, and they will usually contact the breeder first. I have picked up many great dogs this way.

Other reasons the breeder will have an adult dog for sale is as follows:

1. The breeder decides to keep a puppy and it fell short of their expectations in show or obedience.
2. The breeder was unable to sell one or more of the pups so they kept them for twelve months, then advertised them.
3. Breeder downsizes their breeding stock.
4. Breeder gets a better stud dog and sells off the old one.
5. Breeder raises pups to sell as high price working dogs.
6. Breeder sells dog on behalf of other club members.
7. Breeder is also a dealer or trainer.
8. Breeder sells rescue dogs.

Some people in the industry will call themselves breeders but in actual fact they are puppy farmers and adult dog dealers. Some questions to ask the breeder over the phone are:

1. What is the history of the dog?
2. Why is the dog for sale?

3. How many owners has the dog had?
4. Is the dog vaccinated, wormed, and health checked?
5. Has the dog got pedigree papers and a microchip?
6. What is the dog's personality like?
7. Is the dog from show or working lines?
8. Can I see the parents?
9. Do you know of any bad behavioural or medical problems?
10. What training has the dog had?

If you're happy with the information so far and you decide to make an appointment, ask for the breeder's email and list all the questions for the breeder to confirm. As an example:

Dear Breeder,

Thank you very much for taking the time to talk with me and answer some of my questions over the phone. As discussed I would like to confirm the following you told me over the phone. The dog is a German shepherd male, two years of age and not de-sexed. You bred the dog and it was sold at eight weeks of age and returned last week at two years of age as the owners were moving. The dog is currently vaccinated, wormed, and pedigree papered, and you have the paperwork in regards to this, which will be supplied with the sale of the dog. You know of no medical problems and the dog is a good watchdog. Total price for the dog is $1500 with the paperwork.

If you can email me confirmation of the above and also confirm the time we arranged to be at your home No. 69 Breeder Ave. Dogsville.

The above sample letter will at least give you something in writing and you will have a record. I have seen so many disputes between breeders and buyers, so at least do the basics to cover yourself.

My Ultimate Dog from a <u>Professional Dog Trainer</u>

I will try to be as unbiased as possible and give a balanced view as I have been a professional dog trainer for over thirty years. I have seen some brilliant dog trainers that are greedy and rip people off and some very average trainers that are honest and try their best.

Getting your dog from a professional dog trainer is by far the best option as the trainer will select good dogs and do lots of training before having the dog up for sale. You can also just leave it to the professional dog trainer to get your ultimate dog. A bit of insight into the professional dog training world will help you understand the best way to secure your ultimate dog from a trainer. In Chapter 7 I cover with more detail the different types of trainers.

Professional dog trainers can work out of boarding kennels or from their own home. Dogs they secure many be on a large scale of imported dogs or locally sourced dogs. Some facilities may have over fifty dogs in training and several trainers while others may only take on two or three dogs.

When you know the type of dog you want and the type of training, such as obedience or protection or detection work, then you can start the search for dog trainers that train in those areas. To locate a dog trainer check out online pages such as Facebook and YouTube and look for reviews from past clients. I also recommend you speak to local animal control and other dog groups for more info.

This is where it gets a little bit tricky. Just about every dog trainer is in a dog trainers' association that may be for obedience trainers, positive-only trainers, balanced trainers, law enforcement trainers, etc. This is where you will get so much conflicting information on which trainer is the best. Unfortunately in some areas the professional dog training industry is rife with big egos, backstabbing, and professional jealousy. With research you will be able to narrow it down to a few trainers who will be able to provide you with a potential dog. Trainers will bring in dogs from so many different backgrounds, from imports into the country to flying dogs interstate or picking up local dogs. The dogs they take in may be giveaways from family homes due to behavioural problems. They may pick up dogs from the pound or a rescue group, or they may have a network of breeders that they secure returned adults from.

Some trainers will even raise a dog from a puppy. The quality of dogs will vary greatly, with types including retired security patrol dogs that may be six years old to dogs that are as young as fourteen months old with great potential. The professional dog trainer will take advantage of highly trainable dogs and usually keep the dog for more advanced training and to be sold for a premium price.

The best way to deal with a professional dog trainer is to call and ask what they have available and explain to them exactly what you want in a dog. If the trainer has not got what you want, then ask if you can make an appointment to see them. This will give you a chance to check out the facilities and maybe see a demonstration of other dogs the trainer has available.

You may find that the dogs or the training are poor quality, or you may be very impressed with what you see. If you can sit down with the trainer and give them all the details of what you want in a dog and the training required, you can be contacted when a potential match comes in. When you view the dog and find it is exactly what you want you may then work out a training program with the trainer of how you want the dog trained. At the end of the training program, which may last just one week of in-kennel obedience or six weeks of advanced training, you will be able to see a demonstration of the dog working and you'll receive handler training and introductions.

This way is by far the easiest way to get your ultimate dog, providing you have a good relationship with a quality professional dog trainer. You may even find your dog elsewhere and take it to a professional dog trainer for testing and training.

In Chapter 7 I will cover some more details on the different types of dog trainers and dog training services available.

Gaz Jackson

Checklist and Questions for the Seller

I have covered some places where you may find your ultimate adult dog, from classifieds and the internet to breeders, welfare groups, and professional dog trainers. Wherever you find your dog you will still need to tick off a checklist of questions you can ask the seller. Questions will vary in some areas depending on whether the seller is a welfare organisation or a trainer.

History of the Dog

Try to get as much information as possible with regards to this, as in some cases the seller has little to no history on the dog. Find out if the dog came from a family home and how many homes the dog has had. The dog may be very destructive and have been sold several times before. You don't just want the seller telling you about the dog's last loving home and not mentioning the four before that. Ask the seller about the breeder of the dog, what age it went to its first new home at, and what the family was like. In a lot of cases the seller may not know many of these things, but always ask. Ask if the dog is currently vaccinated and wormed and ask to see the vaccination card.

Take note of the veterinarian on the card as you may be able to ring the vet to get more information on the dog. You will be surprised at how much additional information you may get from the vet, such as the dog's true age, which the seller might not tell you. Medical and injury history is another big one as you may find out the dog in the past has been hit by a car and had major surgery or the dog was diagnosed with hip dysplasia or another medical condition.

Ask why the dog was for sale from the previous owners; maybe they were moving, or maybe the dog was out of control or bit a person. Also ask how long the seller has had the dog as some dogs are hard to sell due to looks, age, or behavioural problems, so the dog may have been there for months.

Demonstration of What the Dog Understands

The seller should be happy to do a demonstration of the dog working in obedience and other areas the dog has been trained in. Welfare organisations may have inexperienced staff that do not know the dog and may only just stand and hold the lead. If the dog is from a trainer then ask to see a demonstration of the dog in the areas it has been taught. Also ask the seller if the dog can be walked around other dogs and people so you can see its reaction. Many dogs are so sweet until you show them another dog and they turn into a killer.

Paperwork of the Dog

To avoid buying a dog with papers or a vaccination card that you never receive, try the following.

Ask to view the pedigree papers and vaccination card of the dog. In most cases the people that distribute the pedigree papers require the seller to submit them. Many don't or forget or move or tell you they have been mailed and you will never see the pedigree papers again. I always tell the seller I will submit the papers myself and have them sign the back to prove they know I have them.

If you get the story that another party has the papers and the seller cannot show you then I will ask the seller to put it in writing that the dog comes with papers and a timeframe of when I will receive them. I also tell the seller I can come back and pick them up. One statement that will always get the seller squirming is, 'If I take the dog today when it is un-papered, I'll take it at an un-papered price and pay you the balance when you get the papers.'

If no vaccination card is provided, ask for the dog to have fresh vaccinations or for the seller to provide you with the veterinary contact details so you can confirm and get a copy. If the seller cannot provide you proof of vaccinations then you can ask to take vaccination cost off the price of the dog. Some sellers say their vet supplies them with the vaccinations and they do it themselves and that's why there is no record. Tell the seller that you have to put the dog in a boarding kennel and you do require the vaccination card.

Ask to have all the details on the receipt, from vaccination card, microchip, and pedigree papers to full details of the dog and training. Also have on the receipt the seller's guarantee for health. Whatever they tell you when they're selling the dog to you, get it in writing on the receipt. Also ask if you can have a fourteen-day trial period so that if the dog does not work out you can bring it back.

When I was operating a large dog training centre I always ensured that the clients were happy and had excellent follow-up service. Here are some of my guarantees on the sale and training of other people's dogs:

- All clients that brought dogs in for a seven- or fourteen-day obedience programme only paid in full on completion of the program, after seeing a full demonstration when they picked up their dog.
- The owner was trained to handle the dog and we gave free phone support for any future problems.

- I gave unlimited free dog training private lessons for any problems our clients were having with dog obedience.
- On the sale of dogs we put on a demonstration and then conducted the handler introductions. The owner paid for the dog in full and that was put in a separate account for fourteen days. For the first fourteen days of ownership the new dog was on trial to ensure the owner was happy. If the owner wished to keep the dog then we credited him with several handler private lessons and a seven-day in-kennel training program for the dog in a few months' time. This allowed the new owner to come back and say, 'Here is a list of the dog's problems at the moment' so I could refine the dog's training.
- If the owner changed their mind or the dog did not fit into the household then I gave a full refund on the return of the dog less a private lesson fee for the demonstration and introductions.

There are also laws that protect the consumer, so if the product is falsely advertised, faulty, or misleading then the consumer is entitled to repair, exchange, or refund in most cases. Dogs under law are a product.

Chapter 6

Adult Dog Tests

I am in the north of India near Nepal as a volunteer for Veterinarians Without Borders, helping out the street dogs of Sikkim. I have spent my time off touring Buddhist temples and meditating. I am writing this chapter from one of the oldest Buddhist temples in Sikkim, with monks chanting around me.

***

The first step is to ensure you know exactly what you want a dog for. You may want your dog as a pet or family guard dog, or as a working law enforcement dog. Others may want a detection dog or you may just want a dog with training potential so that you can resell it.

In the last chapter I spoke about all the places to start looking for a dog, so now you have found one advertised and you want to check it out. Remember to have your list of questions for the seller that covers medical history, why they are selling, etc. In most cases you can determine on the phone if the dog has potential based on the seller's information; if things look good then you can organise a viewing of the dog.

Remember, if you tell the seller what you want the dog for, then they will tell you either that the dog is suitable or that they don't want the dog to go to a home like that. Instead of saying, "I would like the dog to be a family guard dog" ask, "Can you describe the dog for me—is it aggressive, goofy, submissive—and what's it like with other dogs and people?' I will get so much information from this question, then I will ask, "How do you punish the dog?"

The seller may open up, telling you that the dog is great with people and will lick anyone to death, but it doesn't like small dogs and when it's in trouble the owner will yell at it and give it a clip behind the ears.

So this dog potentially has been suppressed, is vocally dominated, and will be hand-shy, scared of raised voices, and also possibly animal aggressive. The dog may be suitable genetically but destroyed environmentally, so it may not be suitable for a guard dog. You may be able to override some of the fears and the dog's ball drive may be excellent in which case it will still suitable for detection training.

I have still gone out to look at many dogs I believed were write-offs on the phone and some I have purchased and they turned out great. Others have been a waste of time, so prepare to view several dogs before you find the right one.

When I make an appointment to view an adult dog I will get there as soon as I can— as most dogs are sold straight away, you will miss out if you're late. After I have got most of the information from the owner I will request the following: "I would love to see what the dog is like if I just approach without the owner there so I can see its personality. Is it possible you can have the dog in the yard, and don't feed the dog before I get there?" The reason for this is that the influence of a dependent or overprotective dog on the owner is huge. With the owner holding the dog on-lead or in the front yard, the dog may have enough confidence to run at the fence and aggress and look strong and confident. Without the owner there, the dog may do nothing or hang around the door or show a playful submission. So you may get two totally different reactions from the dog depending on the owner's presence. With the first response mentioned, with the owner there, you may pass the dog for protection and fail the dog for detection. With the second response mentioned, without the owner there, you may fail the dog for protection and pass the dog for detection.

In my next book I will be going into extensive detail on dog evaluation and psychological profile charts and testing for many types of dogs for training or rehousing. When you look at an adult dog in most cases you are limited to the amount of tests you can do at the dog's home with the owner there. Some owners don't take it too well if you show up with a body bite suit for a full evaluation of the dog to see if it is suitable. This is where some more discrete tests can be done to work out the dog's potential. You can also ask the seller whether if the dog doesn't work out you can bring it back in a few days' time, and offer to pay a fee for the inconvenience. Most sellers love this idea as it's the best way to ensure the dog has a great home and is not going to be re-sold or taken to the pound.

When I approach the house I will slam the car door as I'm closing it or whistle so the dog can hear. I will then look for the many reactions the dog has. The reactions may be from no suspicion and ignoring me, to hectic aggression from behind the fence. If I'm looking for a dog for training as a guard or law enforcement dog, I want high suspicion and for the dog to be confident enough to run to the fence barking, with a deep, guttural aggression. Hair standing up on the back occurs when the dog tries to make itself look bigger and it is defensive body language that also comes with a host of other behaviours such as hectic barking and having ears pinned back. These behaviours suggest the dog is defensive with an element of fear-based aggression to the threat. The lack of confidence may be as it is on its own, but different when the owner is with it. If you give this dog a small threat, with eye contact and a sharp movement, then freeze and run away, you will find the dog will chase after you down the fence-line. The difference with the aggression is that the fear will be less and the defence will be a little higher. As you have darted off, the dog's confidence increases and so does its prey drive to chase.

I have seen many dogs that will stand well back in the yard and bark as they lack confidence and yet with a small agitation session of two minutes and a win the dog is a totally different dog.

You may also come across very dominating, hard character dogs that will stare straight through you and give very little display behaviour except a slow walk and deep growl. I find that although these dogs may do bite work they are very arrogant with the handler as they are mostly genetically hard character and unsocialised.

You may find other dogs run up to the fence and are all excited and happy, with a great attitude as well. Many dogs have a great genetic base for protection training but have been well socialised with people, so the suspicion is not there, and this is when you will need to do a suspicion test on the dog to see how it reacts. As you are still on the other side of the fence I would then hit the fence with the back of my hand near the dog and retreat sharply to try to get a reaction, as some dogs may only respond with aggression to a little extra pressure.

Signs of high levels of fear in a dog are hair standing up on shoulders that continues to the base of the tail, hectic aggression with a high-pitched bark or squeal, ears pinned flat against head, peeling the lips up only to show front teeth, or the tail puffed out and erect. Dogs that exhibit these signs may not be suitable for what you want. The fearful dogs will develop a strong dependency and in their own environment may look and act normal, until they are exposed to a new environment or stimuli when they will revert back to being fearful.

Once you have a basic profile on the dog and can establish that the dog is confident or has potential, you can do some more tests to see if it will make the grade.

I would not consider a fearful or highly submissive dog with slow recovery as a candidate for your ultimate dog. Many have tried in the past, and although they may make some progress, dogs like these are near impossible to train as anything more than a family pet. As a professional I can ask the owner to hold the dog on-lead so I can do basic agitation or a stalk test to see the reaction; some will explode with aggression, confirming they have potential for more training. I will not, in this book, show you agitation tests for the dog, as if you get it wrong you may get chewed up due to lack of experience.

Further tests can be used to figure out what drives the dog has for the purpose of training.

You may want a law enforcement dog and find one that has great aggression but the motivation of a wombat, with no food drive and no ball drive, so if you can't motivate it then the training program will fail and most of your training will be about trying to get the dog interested.

The four categories that all tests will fit into are similar to the puppy tests.

1. Positive response to stimuli
2. Fear or nervous response to stimuli.
3. Aggressive response to stimuli.
4. Focus intensity and recovery timeframe.

Again, you can grade the dog how you wish to in each category and the final results provide your full profile of the dog in initial testing. If you are satisfied that the dog has great potential from here, then there is a second series of extensive tests to do as well in the next fourteen days.

Have the owner of the dog perform the first test so you can observe the interaction and also how the dog is treated. You don't want to take food away from a strange dog in case you get bitten, so ask the owner to do it. The below tests will give you either a pass or a fail. If the drive is low and potential is bad, then thank the seller and move on to the next dog. If the below tests are passed, then you can move onto the second tests.

1. Observe the dog's interaction with the owner; is the dog happy, defensive, scared, or independent?
2. Ask the owner to show you any obedience commands the dog may know. You will see how the owner trains their dog and with what equipment, and if they are hard or dominating over the dog.
3. Ask the owner to put the dog in a 'stay' position and walk away so you can see what the owner does if the dog gets up.
4. Ask the owner to raise their hand above their head in front of the dog and swing hand down to dog's face, stopping just short. Does the dog cower, blink, or is there no reaction?
5. Ask the owner to pick up a stick in front of the dog and raise it above their head.
6. Ask the owner to put dog back in 'stay' and approach the dog at a fast pace, front-on.
7. Ask the owner to raise their voice in a deep, guttural manner near the dog. When dogs have been smacked the owner usually raises their voice, walks aggressively to the dog, and smacks it, so the

dog may respond with the same fear to points four, five, and/or six.

8. Ask the owner to get a bowl of food for the dog and place it in front of the dog, then after a few seconds take the bowl away. Does the dog accept this or show aggression and possession over the food?
9. Ask the owner to get the dog's favourite toy and throw the ball for it, to grade the dog's drive.
10. Ask the owner to get a dog rope and play tug-o-war with the dog to grade intensity.

Perform additional tests to check for stability, noise, and touch, and you can get a reading to see what the dog is like with body sensitivity, nervousness, suspicion, and anxiety. There are other areas in behaviour including the different types of aggression, dependency, keenness of the dog to learn, or how stubborn the dog is. If you are looking at dogs that have got aggression then don't do the tests that involve close contact or you may just get bitten.

1. Walk outside the yard and then walk back in.
2. Praise the dog and place a lead on it, then walk back out the gate. This is to see the excitement levels or stress of the dog and focus on the handler or the outside world.
3. Walk the dog past a house that has dogs in the yard to see its aggression level, pulling, sniffing, and body language.
4. If the dog shows aggression, place it in a 'sit, stay' position about twenty feet from the other dog and check focus and response to your commands.
5. Take dog back to the yard and gently run your hands over its head and shoulders and down its

body, checking for relaxing composure to stressed state.

6. Lift one leg up and put it down and stroke the tail.
7. Rub the ears and lift lips or open the dog's mouth.
8. Make a loud noise with a newspaper hitting a wall or table near the dog whilst the owner holds on to it on-lead. This is to test for fear and reaction and, most importantly, recovery time.
9. Open up an umbrella in front of the dog.
10. Both yourself and the owner walk out the front gate, leaving the dog behind to check dependency and stress or barking to get out.

The first ten tests with the owner handling the dog give you an overall profile of the dog and the next ten cover how the dog interacts and tests for stress and being handled. The next group of tests is to check the drives of the dog for training.

1. Throw ball across yard whilst dog is on-lead, release dog after ball has stopped (ball is live prey).
2. Throw ball up in the air or bounce it of a wall, then hold ball to check the reaction of the dog (ball is live prey).
3. Walk around with the ball in your hand held out at around chest height to check if the dog follows you everywhere or leaves (ball is live prey).
4. Check the dog's reaction when you try to take the ball from it. Does it drop the ball at your feet or run away with it so you have to pry it out of its mouth?
5. Hold up a tennis ball in front of you to see the dog's reaction and focus. Is the dog hypnotised by the ball, or only has limited interest (ball is dead prey)?

6. Have the owner hold the dog on-lead as you walk away with the ball and place it down out of sight of the dog. After one minute's wait release the dog to see its interest in dead prey with time factor. You will be checking intensity of search including sight, smell, and speed (ball is dead prey).

7. Place the ball under a heavy pot, bin, rock, or other item with the dog out of sight. After one minute release the dog and say 'where's the ball?'. Check for drive and length of search, if any, as some dogs will only respond to live prey. Check drive for trying to get to ball including digging, chewing, etc. (ball is dead prey).

8. Place ball on other side of fence-line and release the dog to check intensity and timeframe the dog stays at the fence-line (ball is dead prey).

9. Place dog behind fence or screen door and bounce ball off the screen to check intensity and frustration levels (ball is live prey).

10. Have the owner hold the dog on-lead, show the dog a treat and a ball, and walk across the yard, placing them down side by side. Release the dog to see which one it goes for first or if it eats the treat then grabs the ball.

11. Have the owner hold the dog whilst you place a ball across the yard, walk back to the dog, show it a treat, and place several treats before the ball to check if the dog searches for all treats first or goes for the ball.

12. Hold food up near you face to check focus and intensity and timeframe. Give the dog the food to check if it snaps it out of your hand or is gentle.

13. With the dog off-lead, walk around holding food by your left side to check if the dog mirrors your movements.
14. Have owner hold dog on the lead whilst you place food down under a pot or bowl to check intensity and search time.
15. If possible, form large distractions around the dog while you are offering food to check distraction levels.
16. Have the owner hold the dog, then with a dog rope toy, swing it around to check the dog's drive. Let the dog grab the toy and play some tug-o-war to check intensity and fighting drive; let the dog win.
17. Have the owner hold the dog while you stir the dog up with the rope, run across the yard, and have the dog released to see speed and bite on the tug, plus intensity. Let the dog win.
18. Place the dog away for ten minutes, then place the ball and the tug in a tree or at a height just out of the dog's reach. Let the dog out and check for wind scenting, focus, and intensity.

As a dog trainer you have your toolkit of tricks to get the most out of training your dog, which includes treats, toys, leads, etc.; squeaky noises to motivate; hand praise and vocal praise; your body language; clusters of associations; frustration; clickers; and other markers, just to name a few. When you choose a dog with the right genetic base and a collection of natural drives that has been well socialised, you are well on your way to having your ultimate dog.

If the foundation is weak here then you will be fighting a never-ending battle to train your dog, trying to compensate with motivation and confidence building. I have seen many work with unsuitable dogs, and it will only bring heartache as more time is spent developing the dog than training it and in the end you will have a dog with limited potential.

Chapter 7

Dog Trainers and Dog Groups

I am sitting down on the river bank across from the Taj Mahal in India on some ancient ruins. There is a lady in a sari collecting sticks in a bag on her head, repeating the words 'money photo'. I have just returned from Sikkim in Northern India, where I was volunteering with Veterinarians Without Borders helping the street dogs and delivering dog bite prevention seminars for school children.

Introduction to the World of Dog Training

As a veteran dog trainer I have seen many different types of dog trainers and training methods over the years. I will give some general advice on the different types of dog trainers and the methods they use to train dogs. You need to take into account that we are dealing with many types of humans here so we cannot slot an entire group of people into one box. The complex work of dog trainers can be run on greed, ego, good and bad ability, and business ethics. There are professionals and amateurs, part-time and full-time. Although I personally hold a very open view of all training methods, many individual dog trainers will be totally biased concerning their method and believe any other method is wrong.

I believe the easiest way to approach this in the most balanced way possible is to firstly explain a certain type of trainer's methodology and give you the great things about it, then give you the negative side, followed by my professional opinion.

If you decide to get the assistance of a professional trainer the trainer types will now be clearer for you to select who you want to assist you and the methods of training you want used on your dog.

Gaz Jackson

Current or Ex-Service Dog Trainer (Police, Military, Prison)

I have worked with many ex-service dog handlers over the years and they are very experienced in handling and training dogs. They have extensive training for operational duties both in the classroom and field. The service dog handlers are always working in dangerous situations so they have to be excellent at what they do. The dogs they use in the military are selected from some of the top breeding kennels from around the world and many departments have their own breeding programs.

The service dogs are usually German shepherd and Belgium Malinois; these dogs have high drive and hard character so they're the perfect top-shelf dog breeds to start training with.

The facilities mostly are first class and they have a big support crew from veterinary and kennel staff and highly trained military police dog trainers. Handlers have the perfect environment to learn and become a talented handler or trainer in. I have very high respects for these men and women that serve our nation.

When service dog handlers retire and enter the private sector of dog training they will see a massive variation in dogs compared to the dogs they deal with in the services. Most will refer to themselves as an ex-military police dog trainers, but the real position may have been as a handler under instruction of a police dog trainer.

In the service dog handler's career they may only handle one to three dogs in their entire service. All of the dogs are highly driven dogs under the instruction of talented trainers and decoys. When the ex-service dog trainer enters the private dog training industry they will find themselves with so many different breeds and so many different temperaments and many behaviour problems.

The service dog trainer then needs to adapt to the many different types of dogs and this will come over a period of time. The foundation training that was received may have been excellent and so the trainer may use the same methods of correction and raised voice, but it may be too much for many of the private dogs as they typically have softer characters. The best ex-service dog trainers have combined their service career with years of private dog training and the end result is a first class trainer.

Gaz Jackson

Self-Taught Dog Trainer

A large amount of the dog training industry is made up of self-taught dog trainers who may range from having next to no experience to many years of working with dogs in training. Some may have grown up with working dogs and now want to make it a career, while others may have spent a large amount of time watching YouTube and reading books. Others are club people who train their own dog before instructing other people in the club on how to train theirs. The self-taught dog trainer has no formal education in training dogs but relies totally on their own experience and ability.

I started out as a self-taught dog trainer watching other dog trainers who worked for my father's security company, and I watched many videos of famous dog trainers, but even with all this knowledge you have to put it into practice. To be a good self-taught dog trainer you need to do lots of study and also have practical experience with many dogs, as well as a burning desire for the industry.

I have known many trainers who can talk all day about training a dog but who have very little ability to actually train a dog. Most of the self-taught dog trainers are keen amateurs who are involved in club activity or are breeders that dabble in dog training. The crux here is that if you come across a self-taught dog trainer, you have to work out if you can trust your dog to be trained by them, and this is when you have to ask the questions. I also know from experience that many will up-sell their ability by saying they have trained more dogs and over a longer period of time. The line they use in most cases is 'I've been training for ten years'. Often the reality is that they trained a dog ten years ago and have not trained any others since. Most will believe they are an excellent trainer and slander everyone else in the industry.

There are many great self-taught dog trainers and a few bad ones. Here are a few tips for finding out whether they can assist you or not. If you are referred to any dog trainer the first question is, 'Can you tell me about your dog training experience?' The second question is, 'Can you tell me of any formal dog training you have had?' You will at least have some information that will determine if this dog trainer may be able to assist. Some of the common self-taught dog trainers are:

Club Trainer or Instructor

A person who goes to the local obedience school and has a position as a class instructor and also trains their own dog for competition.

Club Groupie

A person who joins several clubs and goes to just about every obedience class, they normally have every know gadget in dog training and a fanny pack full of treats, toys, etc. They target the new people and offer all sorts of advice. Away from the club they are usually in dog training internet chatrooms or watching their latest dog training series online.

Professional Dog Trainer Groupie

These people start out doing private lessons with one trainer then start going to different trainers all to work on their dog. Most of the time these people may be in the security industry so will have interaction with other dog industry people. Many will then try to get a small group of handlers together and start training dogs, helping each other out whilst saving money on the professional fees.

The Apprentice

Although they have no formal training this person is accepted by a professional trainer who will teach them handling and training skills. This person will get real life hands-on experience under the guidance of a professional.

The Balanced Dog Trainer

I first must let you know that I am a balanced dog trainer. In many years of training this name was not known until new types of trainers started to appear with many different methods. It led to, several years ago, dog trainers not being able to just call themselves dog trainers as the public were starting to ask what type of dog trainer someone was and whether they used choke chains, and other questions like this. A lot of this was pushed by welfare organisations and dog trainers' groups promoting their methodology.

The balanced dog trainer is one that will teach the dog boundaries with the use of both praise and punishment. In other words, during the training of a dog the balanced trainer will use food and praise and pats as rewards for the desired behaviours. However if the dog displays an undesirable behaviour then the balanced trainer may distract the dog and continue with positive motivation, but if the dog continues to ignore the trainer then they may give a small correction. The correction used may be a quick jerk motion of the lead that is attached to a choke chain or collar.

With the combination of praise and correction the dog will understand its boundaries. In a ten-minute training session the praise, motivation, and treats may make up over 80% of the session, with another 18% being neutral time (time without any praise or correction). This then leaves only about 2% where the dog may need correction. The balanced trainer will only utilise a correction in a limited manner. This methodology is great for teaching commands such as heel, sit, drop, and breaking from the stay.

The balanced trainer will also not discriminate with any training tool but keep an open mind to all that is available. Many dogs are trained on a collar and others require a choke chain. If you have a hard character dog with high pain tolerance you may decide to utilise a pinch collar or electric collar. In the next chapter I will review all these items.

As an example, if you're working with a law enforcement dog with hard character you may find the drive is so strong to get the decoy that you can give very hard corrections on a collar or choke chain and the dog ignores it so you will need something else to shape their behaviour. Other dogs can have very high animal aggression and no amount of yelling or distraction or offering the dog a treat will stop this, so again, the balanced trainer will use correction methods in accordance with the breed and character of the dog being trained.

If a dog only requires a correction level of a three out of ten and you give the dog a six, then you are being cruel. If the dog only requires two or three corrections in a session and you give it ten corrections, you are been cruel.

The balanced trainer should not be confused with harsh and cruel dog trainers. I have seen a few over the years who disgust me with the level of correction they use. Although they may utilise the same tools as a balanced trainer, their training methods are based on total dominance over the dog. The dog will perform only through fear of being hit or after extreme use of corrections. These trainers normally have limited experience or only see the dog as a commercial product and they will be hard on the dog to get fast results for the client.

In summary, the balanced dog trainer is my number one pick to have your dog trained by for operational work. A dog trained with balanced training will understand boundaries and also establish the dog's handler as the leader of the pack.

Positive-Only Dog Trainer

The positive-only dog trainer will only use praise and treats by rewarding the behaviours they want in the dog and ignoring the bad traits. The positive trainer is against all forms of punishment and correction, so no choke chains and no forms of correction are used.

This methodology has become more popular over the years and is usually pushed by welfare organisations such as the RSPCA and some dog trainer groups.

The trainer will have lots of treats to get the behaviour in obedience they want from the dog, and trainers will use these methods for teaching trick dogs or for obedience competitions. If you have a happy, food-motivated dog, these tactics work well to achieve behaviours with a happy attitude. Positive training will work well in the training of detection dogs, because for a dog to be suitable for detection work the dog is tested for high retrieval drive and food motivation, so rewarding the dog with treats and toys when target odour is located is a good training technique.

Positive trainers, when teaching a dog not to jump up, will turn their back on the dog while telling the dog to sit, then reward the dog with a treat. The positive trainer will always condemn any training method or dog trainer that uses any form of force on the dog.

It sounds great—everyone having lots of fun learning together, so for teaching tricks or detection or obedience and agility in the ring, positive-only training can be very successful.

Now let's look at reality, and I know this will receive some criticism from the positive trainers' camp, but as I said before I want to give you the facts without the sugar coating.

Many dogs today are injured or have been killed or put down as a direct result of positive-only training. Firstly, teaching a dog with positive motivation is excellent training and develops a great attitude in the dog, but this is not the problem. Because the dog is given no boundaries, the dog will respond in accordance to its motivation to treats. The problem is that not all dogs are happy, well-socialised dogs that will do anything for a treat or a toy. The positive methods may be excellent in the dog obedience ring, but in reality it's a different story.

As an example, not one totally positively trained dog will work in a realistic real world environment. Out of the thousands of police dogs and working dogs trained, zero would pass any certification using positive-only training methods.

You may say that dolphins are trained in a positive-only way, and you would be correct; however dolphins are very social animals. They are removed from the wild and placed in isolation tanks, then bribed with food to do tricks. In other words, negatives are placed on dolphins through environmental isolation so that the training can be positive-only.

Many dogs may be animal aggressive or mistreated or not food-motivated. The dog may have anxiety, fear, aggression, dependency, or a high distraction level that will override treats for behaviours.

The most dangerous training methods the positive-only trainers will use is on animal aggressive dogs. I have seen many try to stop this problem, from welfare groups to trainers, and remember, they do not give any correction. The method is typically that when the dog starts aggressing, the trainer tells the dog to sit and distracts the dog with a toy and maybe turns the dog around and walks away. This will not only raise the frustration levels of the dog, but also the aggression. Instead of the dog been sorted out on the spot with correction to stop the behaviour, many sessions of training can be completed without the dog ever being fixed.

Welfare organisations will not allow their staff to use a choke chain so when they try, and fail, with their positive-only methods they then put the dog on medication; then when that doesn't work the dog can't be rehomed and is put to sleep. I have many stories on the failures of the positive-only training methodology being used on aggressive dogs, and I'll share just one more.

A welfare group had a staffy cross that was a beautiful dog but that had high animal aggression. In the time of their positive-only training sessions this cute little staffy cross attacked several dogs, causing big injuries and pain to these innocent dogs. The staffy cross dragged a dog's leg through a cage and that dog was put to sleep due to the injuries. This staffy cross killed another dog. In the end this sweet little staffy cross was put down because they would not consider using corrections to fix the problem.

I have witnessed many animal aggressive dogs that were under instruction from a positive trainer, when after several private lessons the problem was still big. I would come along and in one session, problem fixed. This is because I will use a choke chain and I will give the dog a correction if necessary, so the dog figures out very quickly what the boundaries are. I can teach an alternative behaviour to the same situation. There is a place for positive-only trainers and that is to enjoy their dogs in the obedience ring and doing tricks. When they try to push their methods onto people with aggressive or hard character dogs, however, they are in fact endangering the community.

I have known many positive-only trainers over the years and when they are training with all their positive methods and the dog gets distracted, often they will slip in a small correction or two to enforce the exercise—but shhh, don't tell anyone.

Conclusively, positive-only training has its place and can be very good in shaping behaviours, but you also need balance and to set boundaries for your dog. We now have an entire generation of dog owners brainwashed into not disciplining their dogs, which as a result creates many problems for dog owners.

Competition Sport Dog Trainer

There are many dog training clubs where groups of people meet up on a regular basis to train their dog for competition work and trails. The clubs not only include obedience clubs but also schutzhund, IPO, KNPV, and French Ring. In these clubs dogs are taught very high levels of obedience, protection, and also tracking. The handler will spend months or years training their dog then put the dog through a trail to get a working dog title, which is also reflected on their pedigree papers after the dog's name.

The trainers involved in these organised clubs are extremely passionate about their chosen breed and training their dog to the highest standard and competing against other dogs and trainers. I have found that these sport dog trainers spend a lot of time on personal development as a trainer and the latest equipment that is available. The clubs are very close and all of them support each other to get the best out of their dogs. So the competition sport dog trainers are a very good choice to go to learn skills from to assist you in training your own dog, and also to watch several dogs in training at different levels. I have found that most of the people in these clubs are so passionate about what they are doing that they believe their breed of dog and the sport they are involved in is the greatest on the planet and is far superior to anything else.

When talking to sport dog trainers you will get a one-sided view in favour of their breed and their sport, however, so be aware; you are speaking with people that are very obsessed with what they do.

Remember, these clubs are sport dog clubs, so if you are looking at your ultimate dog as a law enforcement dog here are some things to be aware of:

1. The bite work is equipment-focused so the dog sees the arm pad like a big toy, and this is not going to help you in a realistic situation. If you are being attacked, points count for nothing.
2. Some of the exercises are irrelevant to law enforcement dogs so they are a waste of time and effort.
3. Hold at bay is great in schutzhund but may not be the best for operational work.
4. Dogs in a club environment are relaxed and happy but may be totally different in a threat situation.
5. Tracking may be excellent in a nice grassy area at the club but the dog has no conditioning for real situations.
6. A dog's obedience may be excellent but you don't want this to override its ability for protection on the streets.

I have trained with many sport dog trainers and evaluated hundreds of sport dogs. Many titled dogs were brought to me so the handler could use them as a protection dog; in some cases they have to be retrained from being totally equipment-oriented in prey drive in order to display defensive aggression on the decoy and concealed arms. Using these dogs on the streets without retraining, you end up with a happy, relaxed, confident dog that does not react to many things as nothing bothers it. Some dogs can be trained as sport dogs and they can work on the street without any problems, but it is something to take into consideration.

Another common problem is that the handler does so much obedience work with the dog that it overrides everything. One of the common tests I do is to have the handler put the dog in the stay and walk a few feet towards me. I will have a concealed arm or a body bite suit on, and I will shake the handler's hand before then attacking the handler. In many cases the dog just sat in the stay and watched; these ones that came in just didn't know what to do.

Many years ago I visited a few government dog squad units to sell them body bite suits for the training of their dogs. The units were all issued with arm pads only so all the dogs would only bite the padded arm. When I put on the bite suit and worked some of the dogs, I was able to kick at the dog and no matter what I did the dog refused to bite my leg, instead jumping for my arm. When running away and a dog was sent after me in the bite suit, I raised my arms above my head and the dog just ran beside me and only bit when I put my arm down.

This is not in any way about criticising these units; they were limited with their equipment and this then affected the training. These days they are very advanced with the latest gear and are doing an excellent job.

In another case a dog trained on a body bite suit and sold to Florida law enforcement failed to apprehend a male as he was running down the beach in swimmers.

I have also worked with many titled dogs imported from Germany in the United States. The dogs ranged from IPO and schutzhund titles to several ex-Berlin Wall dogs. Over time, all of these dogs were retrained and sold as certified police dogs to different counties.

In summary, most of the sport dog trainers are very talented and knowledgeable and will be able to assist you with your dog. I highly recommend that you check out one of these clubs and talk to the trainers there. Remember that what they are training for is sport, so always keep this in mind if that is not what you want.

Private Lessons

Private lessons can work very well to help you develop your dog under the watchful eye of a professional dog trainer. When you have done your research on the best type of trainer to suit your needs and you want to do private lessons, here are some tips so that you can get the most out of your trainer.

Some professional dog trainers only train handler and dog in private lessons, doing many each week. It is hard for a dog trainer to remember in detail every lesson your dog has had. Trainers will either give you pay-as-you-go private lessons or package a group of private lessons for you at a discount. The first step will be to make an appointment with the professional trainer to discuss what you want in the training of your dog. In other words, let the trainer know the end result you wish to achieve; once the trainer has this you can both sit down and work out a training program.

Advise the trainer that you can do some of the training at home to prepare for the next lesson. This will save you money by developing the dog instead of having the trainer work on this during private lessons. You will also be able to work out how many private lessons you need to get your required results.

As an example: when a client comes to me and says up front that they want to train the dog up to advanced levels, then the first thing I do is get them to the kennels for a meeting and to evaluate their dog. The dog may be a fourteen-month-old German shepherd that the client wants as a security patrol dog. I will ask a bunch of questions on what the client hopes to achieve. I will then outline a development and training program to be completed in private lessons and by the client at home. I may ask the client to develop the dog's bite through play by playing rag games. The dog may know little obedience and I may tell the client to not do any until we develop some natural drives in the dog. In this case the obedience will be done in a different way so that we can develop the best possible attitude that will work in harmony with the protection training.

I will then go through a full training and aggression evaluation to see what potential the dog has. If the dog has limited potential I will quickly let the client know and give them a confidence development program for the dog that may take a few months to complete before the dog is ready for training. If the dog is a pass, then we start working out a lesson plan and I explain what we will be doing in each lesson. The client is also briefed on what is expected in preparation and during each lesson with instructions on how to handle the dog, praise, and safety.

When the client arrives I will go over what we will be doing with the dog during the lesson and what the client is to do as a handler. On completion of the lesson I again will sit down with the handler and explain in detail how the dog went in training, pointing out the dog's body language and attitude. I will then book another lesson but give the client some homework to complete at home to help develop the dog.

Private lessons are a great choice for training your dog if they are financially viable for you and if you have the right trainer and training plan.

Gaz Jackson

Group Classes

Group classes are an option but I see many more negatives than positives. A group class is controlled by an instructor that may not even be a dog trainer. The class will be a group of four to fifteen handlers and their dogs in a line taking instructions in obedience. Many dog trainers operate obedience classes for the family pet dog, and there are also many dog obedience clubs to assist you with your dog. The clubs are run by keen enthusiasts and amateur dog trainers; in many cases people that start off as clients end up instructing classes. The club scene is best described as too many chiefs and not enough Indians. The club is made up of a committee and they may run forty classes a week and host obedience competitions. Every person you speak to in a club is a self-proclaimed expert on dog training and the amount of in-fighting is high. Now this is not with every club, but personally I would not even consider group classes as an option to train my dog.

In more specialised clubs such as schutzund or KNPV they do a great job, and this is the number one choice of many to train their dog. In several European countries every town has a club and dogs are trained and titled, then sold on to police and dealers. So clubs can work and be very good, but also very bad, so be aware.

I find that if you are doing group classes, firstly, the instructor cannot give you absolute attention with fourteen other dogs in the class. Instead, they will be yelling out 'left turn', 'right turn', 'praise your dog', etc. As a handler you may make several mistakes that will affect your dog and result in slower ability to learn due to confidence issues and poorer attitude.

If I was to, for example, teach the dog to sit and stay in a quiet area, it may take me three corrections at, on a level of one to ten, let's say a level three. I will also use lots of praise, treats, etc. So to achieve this exercise, as well as praise I would give the dog three corrections that are a three out of ten.

Now let's look at teaching the dog the same exercise in a class situation. You show up and your anxiety is high as it's your first night. Your dog smells that you are nervous and becomes defensive. The dog smells many other dogs' fear and is also intimidated by some dogs barking in the distance. The dog also has a scent saturation overload of people and dogs in this new environment. The dog may be able to sit every time on command, but tonight you say 'sit' and the dog just stands there as if it never heard you. You repeat your command and finally correct the dog into the sit. You now under instruction try to teach the dog the stay command.

Because the dog's stress and distraction levels are high, what will normally take your dog three corrections to achieve now has become twenty corrections. What would normally be a correction level of three out of ten is now a six out of ten. So an exercise achieved with three number three corrections has become twenty number six corrections, and carried out with a diminished attitude.

You as an owner have put your dog in this position, resulting in more and harder corrections than what are needed. In conclusion, I disagree with classes when first training your dog; however, once the dog understands the exercises, group classes are then fantastic for conditioning the dog during circumstances of distraction.

Gaz Jackson

In-Kennel Training Program

Over thirty years ago I was training my first dogs for clients with in-kennel training programs of seven and fourteen days. I highly recommend this style of training as a good way to get you started with your ultimate dog, if you choose the right dog trainer and program. If you just want your dog to understand the basics, then this will be a good program and the advantage is that the trainer can be precise with correction and praise and will achieve results much faster than the owner. As the dog stays in the kennel facility this will also break dependency-based problems and the dog will come out for several sessions per day. The average session time for in-kennel training is two or three sessions of around fifteen minutes.

You can also work out with a trainer several courses over a twelve-month period along with you also doing some at-home training. This will be the best way to achieve results.

As an example, first organise an appointment with the trainer to work out a complete training plan. You may have a well-socialised six-month-old dog that you want to train up as a security dog. The age is too young, but you can socialise the pup heavily and develop the drive with rag games so that you have some type of foundation.

The first in-kennel program for your six-month-old pup may be a seven-day course to teach the basics with food training. From here you may spend a month at home after the program maintaining and advancing the training. The second program may be a fourteen-day program when the pup is ten months of age, followed by evaluation and testing when the dog reaches fourteen months of age. If the dog is suitable then the dog may stay in for a seven- to fourteen-day foundation training program followed by a two- to four-week program in protection work. The total amount of in-kennel training may vary from six to ten weeks. This option by far is the most expensive, but leaving your dog with a good professional trainer will get you fantastic results.

On the negative side, I have seen many terrible trainers that will take a dog in, charge a fortune, and the results are pathetic. Others will put way too much pressure on a dog to get a result. Some trainers will also charge full price whether they get a result or not, so it's a good idea to ask before you book. When I take in dogs for any training I have a policy that if I do not get results I do not charge for the training. If I test a dog in protection and pass it then after a week's training the dog is still no good, then I will contact the owner to demonstrate where the dog is up to and explain why the dog failed. I will charge the client the daily boarding rate but nothing for the training.

My advice is to choose a balanced trainer and book some private lessons followed by some in-kennel training. With your work at home you will be getting closer to getting your ultimate dog.

Law enforcement agencies around the world buy their dogs fully trained or train them at their own facility and then train the handler and dog as a team.

By far the easiest way to getting your ultimate dog is to buy it fully trained, and this is a very popular option. Many people come to me and give me a list of requirements for their working dog. The basics are breed, sex, age, and looks they want then the training requirements from green (untrained) to basic or advanced trained. This option is the most expensive, so if you are short on time or ability and just want the finished product, then get a professional to source and train your ultimate dog.

Chapter 8

Independent Review of Dog Training Equipment

I am sitting at the base of a waterfall on a chilly day at Mt Cook on New Zealand's north island. I am in the middle of a sell-out tour of private lessons and seminars for animal control officers and some free seminars for dog rescue groups.

Introduction

There is so much equipment available to dog trainers and handlers that will assist you in training your dog. I want to go over some of the most popular of the vast amount available and give you a balanced view on each product. You will be able to decide which is the best type of equipment to purchase and create a checklist to get each item that is compatible with your dog and training.

When I started out I could not get any decent dog gear so I had a lot of my stuff custom-made to suit want I wanted in my professional career; other items I imported from specialist stores in Europe. I also went out of my way to get the best of the best and the latest designs in everything from collars and harnesses to body bite suits. I soon had a collection of hundreds of dog training items in my equipment room for every occasion and found that many of the items were never or rarely used. So here is some info to help you get the best equipment suited to you.

Pet stores usually sell cheap rubbish made from overseas factory lines, from cheap choke chains to collars that snap in half at the clip. I would stay away from most training equipment from the pet store, but it is a great place to stock up on other items including shampoos, bedding, bowls, and toys.

If you go online you will find many dedicated canine equipment stores that specialise in top of the range law enforcement training equipment, from body bite suits to collars and electric collars, or you can custom-make your own lead and collars to suit your needs. My recommendation is to use a pet store for basics like toys and bedding, and specialist canine stores for everything else except for a few custom-made leads and collars made by a craftsman.

Each trainer will recommend that you should only train with a collar or a choke chain. Others will be disgusted that you use an electric collar or pinch collar so the opinions will be coming at you thick and fast. The reality is, all these items in training can be cruel and abusive, but only if you use them that way. All items in training can be very humane and deliver a great attitude in the dog if used correctly. So it's all about how you use the item in training.

One person may walk their dog on a collar and give the dog over 100 corrections on a walk, while another may have the same type of dog and use a choke chain and give only five corrections before the dog then walks beside the handler for the rest of the walk. Every dog is different and has different pain tolerance levels and different levels of distraction. You may be able to work with your dog on a collar most of the time but on other occasions you may need a pinch collar.

The dog may have a high level of animal aggression or high drive for sniffing the ground and this will play a part in what equipment you will use. If your dog has high food and toy drive then you may be able to work the dog on a collar.

The bottom line is, do not be against any dog equipment; all of the different items if used correctly can be wonderful, but every item is not suitable to every dog.

Here are tips on a few items.

Daily Collar

A collar on a dog is a standard piece of dog gear; in most cases dogs will wear a collar every day of their life. The collar is also used to hold tags with the dog's name and your phone number in case it gets lost. When fitting a collar, ensure it is on not too tight but tight enough that you can't pull it back over the dog's head. You should be able to slide your fingers under the collar, which will be enough space for the dog's comfort.

Before I get into the collars for training I just want to cover some tips on the dog's daily collar. When choosing a collar try to avoid the thick, heavyset leather collars or collars over two inches wide. Dogs that wear these collars can develop hot spots under the collar as the collar can hold a lot of moisture. Dogs can also develop an allergic reaction to some dyes used in the manufacture of the collar. If you have a collar that's on too tight, in extreme cases the collar cuts into the dog's neck and some may require veterinary treatment. There also have been terrible cases where a dog is fitted with a collar that is too loose, and as a result a second dog gets its lower jaw caught in the collar, causing horrific injuries. Heavy duty collars can act as a noose for the dog, with many dogs getting caught jumping over fences and hanging themselves. Other dogs can get their collar caught and as they twist to try to escape the collar twists and chokes the dog.

My advice for a daily collar is to get a cloth collar with a plastic clip of around 25mm wide. If the dog through misadventure gets caught on a fence or with another dog's jaw, then the collar should snap off, saving the dog's life. This is not the same collar you use when training or taking the dog for a walk.

In obedience you can use a 25mm-wide leather or canvas collar clipped to your obedience lead. The ring is the weakest point on the collar so if the ring tears the leather you want the ring to slide and not separate from the collar. Some collars have the ring attached with a separate piece of leather; when this tears you will lose your dog.

In protection I would recommend a 50mm-wide single layer of leather or canvas as a collar. The double layers become very stiff and can be pulled over the dog's head. The inside of the collar can have a felt layer for the dog's comfort and the clips should be heavy duty stainless steel. For safety when working dogs in training or operational duties, always clip your lead to the collar and also use a choke chain for back up. I have seen, many times, dogs aggressing on the lead and spinning around, only to pop the collar. You can also use collars 25mm wide, which are also very strong and are a good choice for operational work. A heavy duty dog collar will outlive your dog and last for twenty years if you look after it.

A collar is a great choice for working with puppies and new dogs to shape behaviour with food and positive motivation. If you have a high energy dog with strong drive you may find you will be giving multiple corrections and the dog just ignores you, so you may need to use stronger corrections with other types of equipment. I will always, with repetition and positive motivation, try to get the behaviours followed by using small then larger corrections using a collar if the dog needs it. This will be done before I move to a choke chain.

If a dog only needs a correction level of three out of ten and you give it an eight, then you are being cruel. You need to evaluate the dog and use only what is necessary and get the balance right so you can achieve results with a happy attitude.

Lasso or Training Collar

The most common types of lassos are those that use the rope with the metal ring on the end, and when I was a kennel operator this was the greatest bit of equipment I had. As I was moving dogs all the time from clients to kennel and hydrobathing, etc., the lasso was very convenient. The lasso is also much safer when handling aggressive dogs; many handlers have been bitten trying to get a collar or choke chain on a dog. I will use the lasso and a stick to place it over an aggressive dog's head in a kennel, allowing me to be at a safe distance on the other side of the gate. In every kennel I have been to around the world from private to government pounds, animal control or military, the kennel staff always have the lasso to move dogs around.

In training the lasso will pull tight on the dog's neck, then release, much the same as a choke chain, so the lasso is a good choice of product that sits somewhere between a collar and a choke chain. When testing out several dogs in protection I have used the lasso, as it was so much faster than fitting each dog with a collar.

Gaz Jackson

Choke Chain

And now the big one, the check chain or choke chain, this is the single biggest argument between all dog trainers. Balanced trainers will use choke chains if needed and positive-only trainers will never use one and tell everyone that they are cruel. The dog welfare organisations will also push to ban the choke chains, using propaganda to define them as cruel. The campaigns against choke chains by welfare organisations have been so big that some companies or individuals of the public will not use any trainer that uses a choke chain. We now have dog trainers that actively promote that they don't use a choke chain with slogans like 'Choke Chain Means Pain' or 'The Gentle Modern Method', etc.

Like any equipment, the choke chain can be cruel or very gentle depending on how it is used. If you place a choke chain on a dog then you go to the park with the dog pulling and choking itself the entire way; this may be considered cruel even though you gave the dog no corrections at all. You may also walk the dog to the park giving multiple corrections to the dog on the choke chain, and the dog keeps pulling. This is because the drive to get to the park overrides the correction given and the dog may not understand why it's getting all the corrections.

The dog will be distracted and excited and maybe feel threatened by other dogs' smells or may be dependent and overprotective on a walk to the park—then the handler is yelling at the dog to heel, and is giving corrections. So in this case the handler has put the dog into this position of stress and mass distraction and as a result the dog cops more corrections. So now the choke chain is being overused due to the handler's mistake of placing the dog in this situation before the dog understands what is expected of it.

When you place a choke chain on a dog, hold one ring and pass the chain through the ring so it becomes a lasso. When you hold the chain in front of your face it should be in the shape of a letter p when you place it over the dog's head. The reason for this is so that when the dog is on your left hand side the chain will always become loose as the ring slides down the chain. If you hold the chain in front of you in the shape of the letter q then when on the dog the ring cannot slide up, so it can choke the dog by not releasing instantly. The choke chain should be loose on the dog nearly the entire time. When you do a training session with your dog on a choke chain, start off in a quiet environment first such as your backyard. You can start off with food training and also high motivational praise to get a happy attitude. You can start the dog off in a sitting position, then start some heeling; in this case you have eliminated a great deal of distraction.

When doing a turn you may crouch down closer to the dog and at the same time say 'heel' or whistle or use food to get a behaviour without correction. When giving a correction with a choke chain, firstly have the chain loose around the dog's neck and with a quick jerk action on the lead snap the lead towards you and release immediately. If the dog is pulling on the choke chain you can push your hands forward, holding the lead to create a loose choke chain for a second, and then snap back. In a ten-minute heeling training session you may have eight minutes of vocal praise, two minutes of physical praise, thirty seconds of offering treats, and the choke chain is always loose for the entire session except for maybe ten corrections, which will account for around five seconds. The correction used is only enough for the dog to learn and should not be overused or severe. The advantage of using a choke chain is that you can precisely mark a behaviour and set boundaries very quickly. Once the dog understands the behaviour in a quiet area, then do the exercises with small, then larger distractions. The choke chain is also so valuable when marking bad behaviour problems such as jumping up or barging in when a door is open. The choke chain is also a great tool for animal aggression problems.

In conclusion, the choke chain is a great tool in dog training if used correctly and is fast and efficient. It can be misused, but that all comes down to the trainer. A lot of dogs don't need to be worked on a choke chain at all, and puppies should not be worked on choke chains. The choke chain can be used on all young and adult dogs from toys to giants. On a puppy I will use a collar, then as the pup gets older I will use a collar and food motivation, then I will use a choke chain to refine exercises and establish boundaries.

Head Halters

The head halter can be a great tool to teach focus and for the dog not to pull on the lead. Many elderly have the head halter on their dogs and they all say it's the only thing that controls their dog. As the dog tries to run forward the head halter will pull the dog's head back, so this will restrict its pulling.

One issue with the head halter is that when a dog is overexcited it can start to walk like a crab, or spin around and pull backwards. The head halter is also the most likely piece of equipment your dog will escape from. I recommend the head halter on beginner dogs and to develop good focus towards the handler. You can guide a dog's head towards you with gentle guidance of the lead and also with food treats. I recommend you use the halter in a quiet area, and also give the dog time to get used to having something strapped to its head. You can also use the halter in conjunction with another lead and collar; this also works well as you have two leads on the dog, one to the collar and one to the halter. The dog may be okay on the lead but just pulls every so often, so instead of a correction on the collar or choke chain you may just give a low-level guidance or correction on the head halter.

Gaz Jackson

Pinch Collar

When I first looked at a photo of a pinch collar back in the 1980s I was horrified, thinking about how cruel anyone had to be to use this. When I first picked one up I was against them immediately— this is because I had no understanding of the pinch collar. I made my opinion based on total ignorance and without research, which is very common in the dog industry.

After watching some old VHS video tapes and reading magazines and talking to different people about pinch collars, my attitude and opinion on them changed. I then purchased some different sized pinch collars and started to use them on some dogs that were in training for personal protection. After fitting the pinch collar correctly I started out with very small corrections and found the dogs responded so much quicker in obedience than with a choke chain. A handler can give a dog a hard correction on a collar with sometimes little to no effect. On a choke chain, a firm correction can be given, but on a pinch collar the correction is so much more gentle. When I take a dog out on a choke chain the dog can start off dragging me down the street, but with a pinch collar I can hold the lead with one finger.

The way the pinch collar works is that it distributes even pressure around the dog's neck without choking the dog. As the dog starts to pull, the pressure increases, so in most cases the dog backs off. I found the big difference with doing obedience with a pinch collar is that I will use less corrections and much lighter corrections and the dogs end up with a much better attitude. I will not use a pinch collar on pups or soft character dogs and even on hard character dogs I will firstly condition the dog and start off with very light correction.

The pinch collar works very well on strong character dogs or dogs with high drive and also outright stubborn dogs that clearly know an exercise but just refuse to do it.

In law enforcement circles the pinch collar is an essential piece of equipment as the dogs in training have very high drive and pain tolerance. A common exercise the pinch collar is used for is to control the dog in a 'sit and stay' position while the decoy is close by or for assisting in teaching the release command in bite work. Dogs in training for bite work may have such a huge drive to chase and bite the decoy that they will deliberately disobey commands because their focus is so strongly on the decoy.

The pain tolerance of the dog also increases massively, so it is common to see handlers yelling at a dog and giving huge corrections on a choke chain for the dog to let go. I have also seen many handlers hang their dog on a choke chain as it's the only way the dog will let go of the decoy. This is where a controlled correction on the pinch collar can work, by twisting the chain so the pinch collar clamps down and the dog releases.

Not all dogs have this high drive and they only amount to a small percentage of the dog population; not all dogs require a pinch collar, but some do, depending on the training. This does not mean that all dogs in training for personal protection must be trained on a pinch collar; many can be totally trained on a flat collar only, but for some dogs you will need more than a flat collar. For problem solving I recommend a pinch collar for animal aggressive dogs to establish a 'sit, stay' position around stimuli.

The pinch collar can be easily misused and the handler can give very hard corrections on a dog that doesn't need them. I have seen a dog on which the owner left the pinch collar, and because it was so tight the skin grew into it and the pinch collar had to be removed by a vet. The same can also happen with a choke chain or flat collar. The bottom line is, use a pinch collar only if it's required; try a flat collar or a choke chain first. Condition the dog to the collar and it will be a great training tool for you, or it could be a cruel tool—it's up to you.

Electric Collar

The electric collar would have to be the most hated tool by a large majority of people, as it is the most misunderstood piece of equipment. Just saying the phrase 'electric collar', you immediately think of a high voltage shock to a poor, innocent puppy dog, and wonder how anyone could be so cruel. You might wonder what purpose such a cruel device could serve and think that the people using it must be reported. Electric collars are banned in many areas and some countries, with RSPCA and other groups actively trying to ban them.

On the other side of the argument, many trainers swear by them and they are an essential tool for training dogs in many different areas, such as search and rescue, police dog training, competition obedience dog training, and sheep dog training.

Everyone has an opinion about the electric collars and most are negative, so now I will try to give you some more information so you can make up your own mind. I firstly will clarify my involvement with electric collars and my opinion on the use of them, then how they can be used and misused.

So here is my professional opinion on electric collars: electric collars are very cruel if used incorrectly, and for this reason I oppose the use of them. However, if the electric collar is used correctly, they are a wonderful training tool that will cut down the amount of corrections used in other methodologies.

I fully support the electric collar if used correctly in training dogs. I first used electric collars in the 1980s, then in 1990 I was trained to use them correctly at West Virginia Canine College. I used the collars on some East Berlin Wall dogs that were imported into America when the wall came down and on several police dogs in training.

I was also trained to use the collars on search and rescue bloodhounds. A trail would be set up for the bloodhound where the track layer would run a mile trail. A second person with a dog on-lead would do a cross track and stand with the dog a few feet off the trail. When the handler and dog came past, the bloodhound went off the track to greet the person and dog, and this is the point when the dog was given a pulse on the collar. The dog immediately showed avoidance and went back onto the trail to follow the track layer. After another session the dog then ignored everything except the track layer's scent and was able to track through many distractions and ignore them all.

In police work the electric collar was a valuable tool for off-lead bite work, giving great control over the dog from a great distance away. Since then I have mostly used the electric collar on dogs with animal aggression problems and this was a great way of solving the problem quickly without creating a bad association with the handler for the dog.

Other dogs I have completely cured of their problems include chicken killers; dogs with dog aggression and people aggression; dogs that are digging holes, jumping fences, eating bait, and nuisance barking; and many more. I have also taught many exercises in training from 'heel', 'stay', in protection the 'release' command, and many more. So I support the correct use of electric collars and I oppose the misuse of them. I will outline some more details so you can make up your own mind.

The collar has a setting of one to six or ten, with one being the weakest. The collar is fitted with a little box around the size of a box of matches. There are two metal probes that stick out of the collar and are around one inch long. When you place the collar on the dog the box sits under the dog's neck so the probes make contact with the dog's skin. The handset has a few different settings so you can adjust the pulse level from weak to strong. When you press the button you have a choice of different types of pulses, from one quick, sharp pulse to a series of mini pulses. The collar also has a praise button that emits a ringing noise that you train the dog to associate with your praise.

In obedience you can use the collar with very small pulses every time the dog leaves the heel position, and use the praise when it is walking beside you. This low-level pulse is much more humane than a person giving corrections on a choke chain.

If the dog has animal aggression problems you can pulse it on or off the lead by setting up a training session. Have a dog behind a fence thirty feet away, and when your animal aggressive dog locks on eye contact with it, pulse your dog. You will find the dog will get the association very quickly.

If you do the same exercise with the dog too close to the other dog then the stress levels of the dog will be high and you will need to use a much higher pulse, so start off at a big distance. In problem-solving you can fit the collar to the dog and watch and wait for it to do the bad behaviour, such as run to the fence and bark or dig a hole, and pulse the dog at the exact moment it does this.

In law enforcement training the collar is the most valuable piece of equipment, giving the trainer greater control of the dog off-lead in protection work, from call off from attack to release from the bite. Most dogs in training for law enforcement have very high drive and high pain tolerance with the desire to bite being huge. I have seen many trainers over the years who have these dogs mid-bite of the decoy and they are hanging the dog on a choke chain or pinch collar to get the dog to release, so this is the drive you may be dealing with. The same dog on the electric collar may just need a pulse or two to release with no other stresses. The dog is then rewarded with a re-bite, and pulsed again to release. After only a couple of training sessions you can yell out 'leave' and the dog releases without the pulse being given.

The collar can also be used on soft character dogs to shape behaviours; in so many ways the electric collar is a great training tool.

Now let's look at a bad side: if the handler turns the collar up too high on a soft character dog, this is very cruel and the result will be the dog yelping. This is the most common mistake that is made with electric collars. If the problem the dog has is stress-related then the collar will just put more stress on the dog.

The collar should only be used by professionals who know what they are doing. If the public use the collar they should go through proper training before use. A person who does research by watching videos and reading books on the correct use of an electric collar will get fantastic results and a happy attitude in the dog, but if you don't know what you're doing then don't use an electric collar until you have some type of training.

Electric Anti-Bark Collar

The electric anti-bark collar is similar to the electric collar, however there is no remote control and the pulse is delivered another way. The collar has two probes that deliver the pulse, and a third plastic knob that, when it detects a vibration, activates the collar. The collar is fitted so this plastic knob over the dog's voice box; when the dog barks the vibrations trigger the knob and a pulse is given. The collar has a cut-out switch so it may only give a pulse when activated a minute apart, otherwise the dog will be continually zapped if it yelps.

I have used these collars for many years and they are fantastic at stopping barking dogs instantly and also fixing animal aggression. When I had dogs come into the kennel complex for boarding the dog may be highly animal aggressive, trying to attack other dogs through the kennel. I would place on a collar and the change was remarkable. The most common reaction was that if the dog aggressed, they felt the pulse and stopped for a second. If the dog then aggressed again and got another pulse, the dog then walked around the kennel and got a drink of water. Aggressed again; got zapped. Then the dog sat quietly in its kennel, but if it decided to growl at another dog it felt another zap. For the rest of the boarding, the dog would not be aggressing any other dogs and in most cases the collar could be taken off the next day. In the dog's brain it created the association between aggressing another dog and pain, and after a few attempts the dog stopped.

Now if you had to do this with a choke chain and lead the dog may associate the pain with the handler; the dog will be great when you're around but animal aggressive when you're gone. Also note that the more you correct your dog and raise your voice, the more unsure a dog will be towards you as its handler. The collar eliminates this with the association of pain being with the aggression rather than the handler.

The barking dog is also the biggest problem for many people and local authorities, so the anti-bark collar is the best and most effective way of resolving the problem fast. The dog may bark through dependency, as it misses the owner, or lack of socialisation and its suspicion levels are high. In both cases the collar will teach an alternative behaviour to the same stimuli. Once the dog gets one to four pulses, the dog will change its behaviour and be quiet.

I also want to point out that both dependency and lack of socialisation are stress-related problems, so even if you fix the barking the dog may still be dependent, which is something that will have to be fixed separately. Other problems such as barking at the neighbour's cat is a perfect problem for the anti-bark collar. I highly support the use of the anti-bark collar on most problem-barking dogs and for use by kennel operators and dog owners.

Citronella Spray Collar

The citronella spray collar sprays a fine mist of citronella that is activated when the dog barks. This is the type of collar that welfare agencies recommend using to stop barking dogs.

Over the years I have seen many clients who say the same thing: "We tried that citronella collar and it was useless, the dog emptied it and still barks." The idea is that when the dog barks the mist of citronella will distract the dog and it will stop barking. Apparently dogs don't like the smell of the citronella; however, I have seen plenty that could not care less. The dogs this collar will work on are dogs with a low-level barking problem, such as the dog that barks because another dog barks. The collar will distract the dog and because the barking was not such a big deal the dog does something else.

If the barking is based on high stress, as in a fear-based biter, in most cases the collar is useless. Highly dependent dogs that stand at the back door and bark are dogs that a citronella spray collar will have limited success with.

There are many items promoted by different groups as highly effective problem solvers, but they never live up to their expectations. I have had several clients that swear by them and they have fixed the problem with their dog, but these are only a minority. Ultimately, citronella collars are a waste of money and you will only see limited or no change in your dog, unless you are of the small percentage of dog owners whose low-problem barking dog is helped by the collar.

Gaz Jackson

Fence Containment Electric Collar

In 1990 I checked out the first electric collar containment system in the United States. I was walking to the home of a police dog trainer who had an imported German shepherd that was certified police dog titled. I have worked this dog on the body bite suit; this was a tough dog called Rambo. As I approached the house it had a totally un-fenced back yard and as I got to the road to cross I noticed Rambo on the back porch. Rambo ran down the stairs, running straight at me, barking and showing aggression. I was frozen in the middle of the road, knowing that this dog was about to chew me up. Rambo ran down the grassed yard to the boundary then just hit the brakes and stopped on the grass six feet in from the boundary and continued barking.

At this point the owner came out and walked to me and the dog stayed in the same position. As the owner walked up to me he said, "You're lucky that electric collar still works." The owner was Mr Wayne Davis, the president of West Virginia Canine College. Since that time I have seen many electric fences installed on properties around the country as their popularity grew. People who have the containment systems usually swear by them.

This is how the system works: the property is set up with a buried wire around the boundary, connected to a box that is linked to an electric collar the dog wears. When the dog gets close to the boundary the collar will make a warning sound and if the dog remains there it will give the dog a pulse. Once the dog understands this it will stay in a totally unfenced area and stay within the boundaries that are set up.

There are also discs available that can be placed in garden beds so that when the dog tries to get into the garden it is pulsed. These systems have been fantastic for people on large properties and I highly recommend them as a containment system. Used correctly, you can have several dogs, large and small, all with collars on, contained to an area you choose. It is important that you train the dog so it clearly understands the boundaries.

The containment system will also come with a dog training video and book to get the best results. Do not simply install the system and put a collar on the dog and let it figure it out itself— this would be cruel. The dog may get zapped and have no idea where it came from and get additional zaps, while other dogs may get zapped and try to run through the boundary.

The people who say the system does not work are the ones that do not train their dogs to understand. Some clients have reported to me that the dog knows it gets zapped, but sprints over the boundary; the reason for this is that the dog was not shown to turn around when the warning beep goes off. Fence containment electric collars are a great system but the training of the dog is an essential part of it.

Leads for Training

Whatever you have securing a dog, whether a collar, harness, or choke chain, they are all secured to you by some type of lead. My preference is a 20mm-wide, 180cm-long leather lead. I choose this as it gives me the freedom to do so much more with a dog including giving it free space to run within a twelve-foot radius. If you want to work the dog on a short lead then all you do is loop the six-foot lead in your hand and it can be any size you want. I find that handlers who choose a small two-foot traffic lead are totally restricted with training options.

In protection I recommend a 25mm-wide leather lead that is 180cm long; the strongest leads I've had have been custom-made with seatbelt backing superglued to one side of the leather. Clips can be stainless steel or brass but you don't have to get the massive clips that look more suited to securing a bull. The clip ring should be large enough to clip the collar ring and a choke chain ring. If the clip ring is too tight then when the dog spins around the clip can open due to the rubbing of the choker chain ring or the collar ring. I also prefer the bottom part of the clip to have a round ring that secures to the leather lead; the tight, flat, square type always seems to tear the leather over a period of time.

When holding a lead in protection situations you pass your right hand through the handle and grip the lead—you can even wrap the lead around your hand a couple of times, with your other hand holding the lead further down. From here you can slide your left hand down the lead and re-grip if needed. The best standing position when holding a dog pulling hard in protection is the tug-o-war stance with your weight over your back leg and knees slightly bent.

If the lead is for general obedience then I try to get the thinnest leather possible of around 15mm wide, and a small brass clip. My custom-made obedience lead is a very short lead of 180mm long and 15mm wide made of high grade Australian leather. I also have used a beautiful thin choke chain that was steel plated and the links slightly twisted so that the ring slid down perfectly. I have had this choke chain sewn onto my custom lead over twelve years ago, and it is still the same lead I use now. This lead has trained thousands of dogs, five to seven days a week.

Out of all the equipment you may have, I highly recommend that you design and have custom made your personal leads and collars with the highest quality leather. My personal leads and collars are Aus Nut leather with seat belt material superglued to the back with a strip of felt. I have brass clips, buckles, and rivets with top of the range stitching that is usually used to secure airbags in cars. I also have my gear leather-stamped and a microchip inserted.

Gaz Jackson

Tracking and Search and Rescue Equipment

If you want to train your dog for search and rescue, here are some tips to assist you in getting the right equipment. Firstly, I have seen many people over the years who want to get involved in this kind of stuff and it can seem like it's a good idea at the time. You have to be very committed in assisting others and spend a great deal of time training yourself to be an asset in search and rescue and not a hindrance. I firstly recommend you join the local search and rescue group for training in first aid, bush skills, and rescue operations before you even consider training a dog to find people. You will also have to ensure you have the proper clothing and survival packs and gather experience from search and rescue groups, including operational experience.

Most are very keen to start with this kind of work and then realise that it is not as exciting as they first thought.

If you've got this side covered and you want to get some gear for your dog, then here is a shopping list to get you started:

- Transport kennel with bowls and canine first aid kit.
- Leads and collars, preferably leather so they don't get prickles stuck in them.
- A ten-metre-long tracking lead, but not made of the soft cloth as it will become full of prickles and will absorb water.
- A harness is also a must, and there are many different types of harnesses on the market. I always had one made of seatbelt material that fitted nicely to the dog with an attached jacket with 'Search and

Rescue K9' on both sides. I also had a light weight harness as well. The dog gear placed on the dog can also be another association or trigger so the dog starts to get keen as it knows what is happening.
- A good set of gloves to avoid rope burn on the lead.
- A fold-up bowl and water and canine first aid kit.
- Other useful equipment can include dog booties, neon sticks, a GPS unit to place on the dog, an HD video camera, etc.

When starting your new puppy in training you may need a puppy harness, scent items, toys, and a food pouch that attaches to your belt. In most cases when training tracking dogs the only gear you need includes a track layer, harness, and long line. If you are doing urban search and rescue for building collapse, then you will need more speciality equipment.

I recommend you talk with search and rescue groups in your area in regards to canine training and the standards they require. If there are no search and rescue groups in your area then do your research online and join a club or association to get more information. Remember, in search and rescue, always follow the instructions of the police and ensure your dog is at an operational level before you volunteer to search for missing persons. People with poorly trained dogs arriving on the scene for a search can be a headache for the highly qualified professionals such as police and search and rescue groups.

Gaz Jackson

Personal Protection Equipment

If your ultimate dog is a law enforcement dog or security patrol dog or even a family protection dog, then you're going to need a decoy. I have been a decoy for over thirty years in the training of law enforcement dogs for families, military, prisons, and police, and the most important part of the training is having a great decoy who has experience and knows what they are doing. This also means that they have the correct equipment for the training of your dog.

In the early stages of training you can develop drive yourself, but as the dog gets older you will need the assistance of an experienced law enforcement trainer. Do not agitate your own dog and do not use an inexperienced person to work your dog in protection as this is the fastest way to wreck a dog. Also be clear on what you want, as there are many sport dog trainers with experience, but you may end up with an equipment-happy dog that will never protect you for real but will run off-lead to bite an arm-pad.

There are several ways to have your dog trained as a protection dog and the most popular is to book the dog in for a personal protection program at a dog training kennel, which may be two to six weeks of full-time training. At the end of the program you should see a demonstration of what your dog has learned and then follow up that training with private lessons.

The other popular way to train your dog for protection is to organise a series of private lessons with a professional dog trainer where you as the owner handle the dog and the trainer does the decoy work. It is important that you have a good decoy and it's also import that the handler knows what they're doing as well, to develop the dog. If you choose this method then you may be the weakest link with your handling skills. The decoy and handler must work beautifully together with the handler giving the correct command at the exact times to coordinate with the decoy's moves.

Verbal and physical praise is also very important for the confidence and development of the dog in training. The handler may have to correct the dog and make 'sit' and 'stay' commands and other exercises while the dog is stimulated by the decoy. The decoy is very important, and so is the handler, so this approach is something you must discuss with your trainer before considering.

If you seek the services of a professional then they should have all the proper equipment to do the decoy work, and you as the owner of the dog may only require handler gear. I would also like to point out that many may claim to be a decoy and really have no idea what they are doing and may only have basic equipment like an arm-pad.

Many dog trainers have different ways of training protection dogs, so here are a few tips before I get into a list of protection equipment. Some trainers will go overboard on the obedience training first, which can diminish drive before it's developed, or have the dog unsure of the handler if it has had continuous corrections. Others will instruct the dog or handle the dog before acting as decoy for the same dog; this should not be done.

Other trainers will do every training session with an arm-pad on and the dog operates with prey drive to get the arm-pad only, so when the dog gets to the training field it sees and smells the arm-pad and then the protection training is just a big game. Many handlers have found this out the hard way when they were attacked for real and the dog did nothing or showed avoidance because it was the first time the dog felt threatened.

Arm-pads should only be used for sport dogs and not for law enforcement training. Work out an entire training program with your trainer that includes evaluation, confidence building, development of drive, raising suspicion level, and bite development. A good trainer should be able to explain the entire process to you so you know exactly what to do as a handler and you will see the dog progress each training session.

Equipment is so important as it has to be safe not only for the dog and handler but also for the decoy. I have had many close calls due to equipment failure or the handler showing up in flip flops or other inappropriate gear.

The first thing is that the handler of the protection dog must have good quality footwear that fits well and has good grip. Ensure you have no loose jewellery or clothing that can get tangled up on the lead or the dog. Plan the session with the decoy first and ensure you know and can understand their instructions.

Another tip: be careful of sunscreen and moisturisers as lotions will make the leads slippery.

As for the standard collar for a dog in protection, I recommend a leather, two-inch wide collar with felt backing. The double layered leather collars become so stiff that they can pop over a dog's head. The agitation collar should only be used in training and not be the daily collar. The lead I recommend is a six-foot leather lead, 25mm wide and stitched. Another great lead is the police dog lead that has two or three brass rings and the handle is formed by securing the clip to one of the rings. The safety advantage is that the dog can be clipped to chain wire fences, if you get a dog that turns on you.

The buckle should be heavy duty with a snap large enough to secure the agitation collar as well as a choke chain for back up. As a decoy working so many dogs I have had several that have aggressed, then spun around, popping the collar off, but as the lead was also secured to a choke chain I was safe from attack.

Some people will use harnesses for training their dogs, but I have never liked using these as a handler and especially as a decoy; the dog has more freedom, which is great, but is more difficult to handle.

The choke chain back-up should be high quality stainless steel, which can be purchased from speciality stores or online. Many pet stores will only stock the cheap, crimped, overseas-made choke chains, and these are very dangerous. Another setup is to have a lead and collar on the dog and a pinch collar with a handle on it, or a small tab lead. This will allow the dog to aggress on the leather collar and when the handler wishes to enforce the leave command they can use the pinch collar if needed.

If you are developing your puppy to be a future law enforcement dog then you will need the puppy leads and collar and to develop the dog's drive with a ball or well-known Kong toy. Rag games are also great as you only have to use a tea towel or sack for tug-o-war games. You can also use tugs that are a rolled up sack in the shape of a tube. Remember: these are just games between the owner and the dog.

Some trainers will start off with a young dog of ten months of age doing rag games, then use the soft sleeve before using a hard sleeve to play as the pup is too young. This will make the dog see the decoy as a game partner and the drive will only be towards the equipment.

The way I have always started a dog out is by doing the evaluation so that the first time the dog sees the decoy the dog feels threatened. I will have no protection gear such as pads, etc., and I will be in street clothes and only carry a stick and a rag. When I do this test I ensure the dog is a young adult of at least fourteen months of age. The dog may aggress and feel threatened by me, not thinking it's play time with the sleeve. After the evaluation, I will do a small agitation session, then finish the training there.

Now we will have a dog that shows aggression to the decoy and is not equipment-driven. With several more sessions the dog will have a serious level of aggression and I still have not shown it any dog gear as of yet. When we get to the bite work I do not use arm-pads at all; I will use a body bite suit. When the aggression is strong towards the decoy then the dog may bite whatever is presented, so with a strong foundation the dog can go straight onto a leg or arm bite in the first training session. I also do more agitation in street gear, then with equipment, so that the dog is targeting me and not just the gear.

So that brings us to the gear you need for protection work. A concealed training body bite suit is the first piece of essential equipment for the decoy. If the decoy is new, or for extra safety, you need some boxes for your hands, and high quality shoes.

The second bit of equipment is a whip or padded stick; this will allow the decoy to crack the whip and whack itself on the leg with the padded stick as part of the agitation. This also allows the decoy to conserve energy during agitation.

A basket muzzle is also very essential to not only teach the dog to bite but also to fight the decoy who will be in street gear. In training you can have the dog knock the decoy down and fight them, then command the dog to lay down next to the decoy so you can frisk and cuff them. The basket muzzle is also great for keeping the public safe not only in training sessions but also if the dog is operational in public areas with many people around. Most muzzles have a quick release so that if a situation develops the muzzle can drop off in a second.

The other essential piece of equipment is a concealed arm— both mini and full arm. This is a tight fit that has a rubber insert and laces up so the sleeve can be worn under a track suit. I have always hated doing decoy work with a concealed arm, as it is the most dangerous and it really hurts. Every time I do decoy with a concealed arm my arm ends up yellow and purple and bleeding. Most decoys won't use the concealed arm because of this reason, but it is great for testing out dogs in an operational environment.

There are many other items on the market, but the above list is enough for a decoy. A lot of decoys are collectors and have a big collection of scratch pants, sleeves, bite suits, muzzles, and many other items for the training of law enforcement dogs.

As well as having the gear, you need to know how to use it. I have seen body bite suits in perfect condition except for one arm ripped apart as the decoy only trains with lower arm bites.

Some police departments are disadvantaged by having to train their dogs on sleeves and when the dogs are exposed to a bite suit for the first time they fail and will not bite the leg or won't bite at all if the decoy's hands are in the air.

Your best option is to seek a professional law enforcement dog trainer that knows what they're doing and has all the gear. Do your research online and with experts in the field and work out what you want as an end result for your dog. Remember, when you train a protection dog you also have to take into consideration the rules and regulations of the local authorities and keep the dog secured in a dog-proof enclosure to keep the public safe from your dog. Proper signs and locks on gates are just some of the responsibilities of owning a dog that bites. So please be responsible and ensure you have all these areas covered.

Handler Equipment

If you are working as a professional law enforcement canine handler in detection or security, most of your equipment will be supplied by your employer. Many of us have to purchase our own gear for training and for operational duties.

I recommend you have some type of training outfit that you wear when you are training your dog; it not only has all your stuff in one place, but it also acts as an associative trigger for your dog. Dogs that are trained in bite work and detection react totally differently when you put on a collar compared to a harness.

When I do my training, although it's easy just to go out in the field in jeans and a T-shirt, this is great for small sessions on a nice day but you will also get rainy days when you will be covered in mud. I have two uniforms that I wear in dog training: if I am doing several sessions a day then I have a lightweight set of overalls I can slip on and off during the day and some slip-on shoes instead of the big, heavy duty lace ups. If I am working with detection dogs I will wear a fishing vest as it's waterproof and has lots of pockets to place all the gear in. I can load the front pockets with specimen containers with target odours and the other pockets can have gloves, a spare lead, a small first aid kit, toys, treats, and anything else you may need in a session.

If I'm only doing a small session or I have another dog being trained on a different target odour, I will also have the fanny pack with target odours in one pocket and rewards in the other pocket.

In the car I always have a training and comfort duffel bag that is filled with bowls, water, jacket, leads, collars, choke chains, a first aid kit, and spare overalls.

All of the specialist training and operational gear can be purchased online, with a massive selection available for detection, search and rescue, and protection. There is also a big selection of professional handler gear, from tactical clothing to gadgets. Speak with your local professionals in your area for some more advice on what you need in training and operational gear.

Other Items of Use

There's plenty of information to start setting yourself up now and into the future with all your dog gear. Here is your checklist:

1. Home setup for your new puppy or dog.
2. Fences and signs.
3. Puppy training equipment.
4. Adult dog training equipment.
5. Canine duffel bag for car.
6. Dog training kit for home.
7. Operational work-wear for canine.
8. Handler gear for training.
9. Handler gear for operational duties.
10. Specialty dog training gear e.g. for search and rescue or protection.
11. Vehicle setup and transport cages.
12. First aid kit.
13. Registration with local authorities.
14. Medical requirements and microchip for identification.

Please Use Common Sense

I have covered so many different items for the use of training your ultimate dog, but that does not mean that you just use any item I have talked about here. As a trainer the first thing you need is to be compassionate and not be hard on your dog. I have described here giving dogs corrections, and the uses of different equipment. All of the equipment used can be cruel if used incorrectly, and very humane if used correctly. It is up to you to educate yourself and only use what is necessary for your dog and your training requirements. If you can do all the training with food and praise, then do it; you can refine your methodology later with some types of enforcement if you wish. You can train a dog on a collar and you may not need a choke chain or pinch collar for your particular dog, so if you don't need it, don't use it.

I have seen many abusive trainers over the years that will get frustrated with their dog and give unnecessary hard corrections and even hit their dog. Dogs can be vocally dominated and scared of their owner via only raised voice. As a trainer, you have to understand the basics of training a dog, so although some people will oppose the use of some equipment, I oppose the misuse of any force on a dog. I have seen trainers that are against choke chains and will only use a flat collar, but then give their dog very hard multiple corrections. I have seen trainers scruff their dog's neck and yell at them and give over fifty corrections on a walk to the park using a flat collar. I believe this is absolute cruelty and abuse due to the lack of ability and short temper of the handler.

So whatever you use to train your dog, ensure you understand what you wish to teach the dog and use the correct tools for training (which includes praise, treats, and the gear required for your dog).

Gaz Jackson

In the end, the most important piece of dog training equipment is the handler. Work on being the best handler you can be by reading books on the subject of dog training, watching videos, and talking to professional dog trainers or dog training club enthusiasts. All of these things will assist you to develop your methodology in training your ultimate dog. With a clear vision you can develop a happy, motivated dog that loves working with you and tries so hard to please you. An educated handler with clear goals will get great results, so work on you first, and seek a professional to assist you.

About Gaz Jackson

Gaz Jackson was born in Brisbane, Australia and during his childhood had a great interest in dogs as his father operated a security company with guard and patrol dogs. Gaz started off as a child hosing out the guard dog kennels and watching a dog trainer come in to train the guard dogs with sacks wrapped around his arms and, later, cricket pads on his legs.

At the age of fifteen Gaz was involved in a dog training centre start-up business employing a Dutch dog trainer. Gaz spent the next three years helping out by agitating dogs and watching the obedience training.

Gaz decided then that he wanted to be a full-time professional dog trainer and although his relationship with his father was rocky due to a recent divorce, he decided to call him to ask if he could teach him how to train dogs. Gaz's father decided not to teach Gaz, as there was still some hostility. This became the one thing that changed the course of Gaz's life.

Gaz slammed down the phone and made a commitment on the spot, yelling out, "I am going to be the greatest dog trainer in Australia!" and that is where Gaz's professional career started.

Gaz then purchased dog training equipment from around the world, including body bite suits, rattle sticks, muzzles, and tracking and obedience gear. Gaz then purchased dozens of VHS videos on some of the greatest dog trainers in the world and spent many hours watching videos, then putting what he learned into practice.

At the age of nineteen Gaz was training six to ten obedience dogs per week in a seven-day program, including a demonstration to the owners on completion. Gaz was also selling security patrol dogs locally and overseas and conducting many private lessons each week.

At the age of twenty-one the family property was sold and the family trust purchased an established boarding kennel and dog training centre. In the same year, Gaz travelled to America and completed a three-month dog training course in obedience, tracking, and protection at West Virginia Canine College.

Gaz learnt from the best dog trainers from around the world in the videos, and from his experiences at the Canine College, at seminars, and as a dog trainer, he realised the full potential of what you can achieve. Many of the local professional dog trainers just seemed so basic in their in training and knowledge.

Over the next few years Gaz became one of the top dog trainers in the state of Queensland. As a guard dog trainer it seemed the entire industry looked down on him, but as his profile grew so did the professional jealousy within the industry. Gaz then decided that he would turn his back on the dog industry and become a recluse, knowing he was ethical, treated dogs and people well, and would continue with his dream of being the best in the country.

Gaz then ran dog training seminars featuring some of the world's top dog trainers, attended by dog trainers around Australia and overseas. This gave Gaz extra one-on-one time with some of the best dog trainers in the world and brought him closer to his dream of being a great dog trainer.

Gaz's expertise continued in other dog training areas including training search and rescue bloodhounds and locating missing persons and escapees. Gaz then trained Australia's first cadaver dogs and was used in many police and private cases, including the infamous backpacker murder investigation in New South Wales.

Gaz then trained Australia's first private drug detection dogs and conducted private searches for schools and parents of teenage children. At the same time Gaz had a weekly TV segment on dog training on the 10:30 today show and the Ernie and Denise morning show.

Gaz also hosted a radio show on dog training for four years and produced the DVD *Dog Training with Gaz Jackson*.

To date, Gaz Jackson has trained in excess of 20,000 dogs in obedience, protection, or detection, supplying canine and handler training to police, army, prisons, air force, and state and federal agencies internationally. Gaz has conducted several law enforcement dog training seminars with international speakers and patrons. Gaz is an international speaker conducting seminars, events, workshops, and lectures, training handlers and trainers around the world in all aspects of dog training.

Gaz Jackson's Career Achievements

- Trained the world's first megafauna fossil detection dog.
- Trained the world's first water dragon egg detection dog.
- Trained the world's first bio-archaeology dog.
- Trained the world's first quoll detection dog.
- Trained the world's first and second koala detection dog.
- Trained the world's youngest narcotics detection dog at eleven weeks of age.
- Trained the world's first pygmy blue tongue lizard detection dog.
- Trained the world's first slider turtle and egg detection dog for Queensland Department of Natural Resources.
- Trained the world's first three cane toad detection dogs for WA Department of Environment and Conservation and for the region of Groote Eylandt.
- Trained the world's first tobacco contamination dog for Phillip Morris.
- Trained Australia's first operational cadaver dog and worked with state police departments for body searches.
- Trained Australia's first private narcotic detection dogs.
- Trained Australia's first cancer detection dog.

Presentations and Public Appearances

- International guest speaker, New Zealand 2014 54th annual NZIACO Conference. Dog evaluation and dog bite prevention 2014.
- Two national New Zealand tours of twenty presentations.
- India dog bite prevention seminar series 2014.
- Key speaker K9 Conversations dinner Sydney 2014.
- Guest dog trainer Lackland air force base San Antonio Texas USA 2013.
- Key presenter Migaloo and Chance Dog Lovers Show Melbourne 2013.
- Guest speaker Australian K9 sports centre 2013.
- Speaker Sunshine Coast Regional Council Animal Control Officers 2013.
- 2013 Law Enforcement Decoy Seminar.
- University of Queensland archaeology class 2013.
- Lions Club Kallangur 2013.
- Lions Club Burpengary 2013.
- Guest speaker, North Lakes Community Women's Group. Detection Dogs 2013.
- Guest speaker, Logan Eco Action Festival 2012.
- Guest speaker, North Lakes Community Women's Group. Detection Dogs 2012.
- International guest speaker New Zealand 2011 50th annual NZIACO conference. Dog evaluation and dog bite prevention.
- International guest speaker New Zealand 2010 49th annual NZIACO conference. Dog evaluation and dog bite prevention.

- Key presenter, pet expo, Brisbane Convention Centre, 2003. I spoke on several dog-related subjects and provided an aggressive dog demonstration.
- Key speaker, National Animal Control Officer Conference, Pine Rivers, 2001. I provided a lecture and demonstration of several aggressive dogs and how to avoid being bitten.
- Speaker, University of New England, Armidale NSW 2011. Lecture and demonstration on dog behaviour and training.
- Speaker, University of Queensland, Campas 1993. Lecture presentation for vet students on dog behaviour.
- Speaker, Captain James Cook University, Townsville, 1992. Lecture presentation for vet students on dog behaviour.
- Speaker, Work Cover Queensland, Brisbane 2000. Provided several dog bite prevention seminars.
- Speaker, Energex, Brisbane. Provided several aggressive dog demonstrations for dog bite prevention training.
- Speaker, National Dog Trainers Federation, Melbourne. I provided a one-day detection dog trainers' seminar.
- Speaker, Brisbane City Council, Brisbane 2002. I provided training for 100 animal control officers.
- Speaker, Caloundra City Council, Narangba, 2004. Dog bite prevention training.
- Seminar, Origin Energy, Brisbane 2004. Dog bite prevention seminar.

- Speaker, Royal Brunei Gurkha K9 Military Unit, Brunei, 2000. I provided a seminar on police dog training and tracking dogs.
- Speaker, Columbus Police Academy, Ohio USA, 1990. I provided a lecture and demonstration of police dog training and criminal apprehension.
- Host/instructor, Singapore Civil Defence Force, Narangba, 2002. I provided a twenty-one-day explosives canine handler training program.
- Host/instructor, MNK9 Police Dog Seminar, Narangba, 1991.
- Host/instructor, MNK9 search and rescue, cadaver, arson, Noosa 1992.
- Host/instructor, MNK9 100-hour dog trainers' certification program, Narangba 1993.
- Host/instructor, MNK9 protection dog and decoy seminar, Narangba 1994.
- Host/instructor, MNK9 KNPV Dutch police dog seminar, Melbourne 1995.
- Demonstration, NSW pest animal control conference, Coffs Harbour, NSW 2005. I provided a demonstration of the world's first slider turtle detection dog locating turtle eggs.
- Demonstration, R.A.A.F. Amberley, Amberley Air Force Base 1995. Demonstration and supply of body bite suit for the use of police dog training.
- Demonstration, Queensland corrective services, Wacol 1995. Use of a body bite suit for police dog training.
- Demonstration, Australian Army MPD, Narangba 2008. Providing decoy demonstration skills and talk.

Training

- 600-Hour Professional Dog Training, West Virginia Canine College, Buckhannon West Virginia, 1990.
- Nine Presenters Course, Channel 9, Mt. Coot-tha, Queensland, 1997. Covering voice, movement, script interpretation, appearance, makeup, auditions, auto-cue reading, technical matters, and on-camera presentation techniques.
- Safe Handling and Usage of Explosives, Explosives Training Australia, 2002.
- Certificate IV in Training and Assessment (TAA40104), Australian Institute of Industry and Training.

Talent

- Win news koala detection Noosa council.
- Totally Wild Migaloo Archaeology detection dog.
- Weekend Sunrise Channel 7, koala detection dogs.
- Today Tonight Channel 7, cancer detection dog.
- Weekend Today Show, Migaloo the archaeology detection dog.
- Eukanuba Extraordinary Dogs, cane toad detection dogs, Groote Eylandt, 2011.
- Dog Training with Gaz Jackson, host, director, and scriptwriter, multinational K9 1995.
- Narcotic searches with eleven-week-old pup, host, director, scriptwriter, multinational K9 2001.
- Ernie and Denise Morning Show, weekly dog training segment, Channel 9, 1995.
- 10:30 Today Morning Show, weekly dog training segment, Channel 7, 1995.
- Brisbane Extra, obedience training, Channel 9, 2006.
- Totally Wild, slider turtle detection dog, Channel 10, 2005.
- Australia's Most Wanted, cadaver dogs, Channel 10, 1993.
- Ray Martin Midday Show, cadaver dogs, Channel 9, 1994.

Gaz Jackson

Acknowledgments

I would like to thank all the people who believed in me and have assisted me in my dog training career over the years. From my family and close friends to the many clients, dog trainers, and other people who assisted me and didn't even know it.

Thank you to everyone who inspired, educated, and encouraged me in the wonderful world of dog training.

I dedicate this book to my three wonderful children Clint, Alicia and Lillie-Rose.

Contacts

Gaz Jackson Dog Trainer, International, Speaker Author
For more information contact Gaz or visit one of my websites.
1. Book Gaz for a home private lesson Australia wide.
2. Book Gaz for a home private lessons overseas.
3. Gaz Jackson on demand Book Gaz world wide for a private lesson or seminar within 48 hours.
4. Dog Training tours across Australia and New Zealand.
5. Dog Bite Prevention seminars for animal control officers and industry.
6. Dog training and behaviour seminars for dog training clubs and groups.
7. International speaker for corporate events, seminars and workshops.
8. Independent evaluation and temperament tests for training, legal and safety applications.
9. Validation of dogs for sale for potential buyers from dog training, paperwork and quality.
10. Speaker for charity events to raise money for the charity and train the volunteers.
11. Mentor for dog trainers from careers to operational commercial training.
12. Volunteer for rescue groups to assist homeless and street dogs around the world.
13. Instructor for law enforcement dog and handler training for government and private organisations.
14. Media events for charities.

Gaz Jackson
P O Box 535 Kallangur, Queensland Australia 4504
0419773022
www.gazjackson.com
info@gazjackson.com

www.ingramcontent.com/pod-product-compliance
Lightning Source LLC
Chambersburg PA
CBHW051955090426
42741CB00008B/1407